Extreme Lo-Carb Meals on the Go

Fast and Fabulous Solutions to Get You Through the Day

Sharron Long

Adams Media
Avon, Massachusetts

Published by Adams Media,
a division of F+W Media, Inc.
57 Littlefield Street, Avon, MA 02322. U.S.A.
www.adamsmedia.com

ISBN 10: 1-59337-214-0
ISBN 13: 978-1-59337-214-9
Printed in the United States of America.

10

Library of Congress Cataloging-in-Publication Data
Long, Sharron.
Extreme lo-carb meals on the go / Sharron Long.
p.   cm.
ISBN 1-59337-214-0
1. Low-carbohydrate diet--Recipes. 2. Make-ahead cookery.
3. Quick and easy cookery. I. Title.
RM237.73.L663   2004
641.5'6383--dc22   2004013273

This publication is designed to provide accurate and authoritative
information with regard to the subject matter covered. It is sold with
the understanding that the publisher is not engaged in rendering legal,
accounting, or other professional advice. If legal advice or other expert
assistance is required, the sevices of a competent professional person
should be sought.

—From a *Declaration of Principles* jointly adopted
by a Committee of the American Bar Association and a
Committee of Publishers and Associations

Many of the designations used by manufacturers and sellers to distinguish
their products are claimed as trademarks. Where those designations
appear in this book and Adams Media was aware of a trademark claim, the
designations have been printed in initial capital letters.

This book is available at quantity discounts for bulk purchases.
For information, call 1-800-289-0963.

This book is dedicated to my fathers.
One father, though passed on, is resting in the
arms of my other Father, who is always alive.

"My purpose is that they may be encouraged in heart."
—Colossians 2:2

Contents

Acknowledgments

"Give to everyone what you owe them . . . give respect and honor to all to whom it is due." —Romans 13:7 NLT

Thanks!

Thanks to God for making this possible. I never dreamed four years ago that I would be doing this!

Thanks to all my faithful recipe testers. As with all of my books, each recipe has been tested in the kitchen of real families. Special thanks to Connie Pritchett who has now helped me on all three of my books. Thank you, thank you to Lori Rainey for putting up with me and for coming through in the pinch so many times. Thanks to the many folks from the *LowCarbEating.com* community for helping me out: Rob Bolton, Maggie Fries, Beth Simmons, Barb Keith, Ginger Boucher, Cassandra Hall, Aaron Paden, Jennifer Pond, Donna Bales, Shelley Gattenby, Becca Meixner, Karen Darling, and Carol Robinson. Thanks to Chef Trina Nelson for her contributions.

Thanks to my family for supporting me through this project.

Introduction

Why this book? Here's the answer: change. That is what life seems to be all about. We change our hair and our makeup to fit the latest trends and styles. We change our wardrobe so we won't be "out of date." We change our supplementation routine to gain more energy or just because we know it is good for us. We exercise, hoping to change the effects of gravity. We change our way of eating in order to lose weight and gain health.

Change. Along with all these shifts come changes to our circumstances as well as to our inner self. Vocations change. Homes are bought and sold. Loved ones pass on. New ones are born. We become reflective and change our perspectives.

Change. Life becomes busy. Where once we had too much time on our hands, or at least enough to be able to do crafts, go to yard sales, and enjoy recreational shopping, now the days are full of meetings and activities of all sorts.

Change. With all these changes, how does a person stay true to his or her way of eating? How do you stick with your low-carb diet plan while everyone around you is eating coffee and donuts? I hope to be able to share some insights about what works and what doesn't work, as well as some helpful hints and tips for sticking to this low-carb way of eating for the long haul. After all, this diet is all about changing our perspectives. We've decided that protein and fat are not the negative things we were once taught. We've changed our tastes so that we don't live on bread and refined carbs alone. Now, meats and veggies are our fare.

Each of the recipes in the following pages is labeled with a *Q* or an *M*, or both. This is to help you in your menu planning. The *Q* signifies that the recipe is quick to fix, generally less than an hour from start to finish. If the recipe is coded with an *M*, that means it is one that is meant to be prepared ahead of time to be eaten later. Generally, these are recipes that make great leftovers, or instructions have been given for prepping and freezing the food for later use. If a recipe is marked *Q*, *M*, it fits both of these qualifications: quick to the table and a delicious meal for later! Also, the nutritional calculations for the recipes are figured without any optional ingredients added in, unless otherwise stated.

One final note about the recipes: If you are curious about the term "Effective Carb Count" seen throughout this book, many plans allow fiber to be deducted from the total carb count. This leaves the carbs that will actually affect your blood sugar levels.

I hope that in the following pages you will find some comfort and encouragement that this "low-carb thing" can be done, and in the process discover some really great food as well!

Blessings,
Sharron

Making Wise Choices While on the Go

A few things I've learned along the way.

How can I do all the things required of me, yet still make wise food choices? How can I go to meetings and activities where everyone else is munching on popcorn or donuts and stay true to my low-carb way of life?

These are questions that people who have seriously considered such a lifestyle change must ask themselves. The unprepared low-carber will continually make the wrong choices in these inevitable situations. As a result, he or she will give up in frustration, thinking, *This diet just doesn't work for me!*—when in actuality, the dieter didn't work for the diet.

Before I go on, I want to assure you that I'm not pointing fingers at anyone. Not in the least! I am on this road as a fellow traveler. To be very honest, I did the Atkins diet for nearly two years before I even cheated once. Then, I had a health crisis. I had to go off the diet for several months, and I regained some of the weight I had lost. I tried another low-carb/lower-fat plan. It ended up sparking cravings, and I struggled for several months to stay true to that plan, mostly because I couldn't go back to the higher-fat style of low-carbing. The crisis passed, and I discovered another low-carb plan called the Go-Diet. It is very similar to Atkins, only it emphasizes the use of probiotic dairy foods like yogurt and kefir. Since that health crisis, though, I have struggled to make the right choices. Again, honestly, I've made a lot of bad ones.

Planned Cheats

This low-carb way of life is not a quick fix. If it is truly going to help you stay healthy, it has to be a way of life! Yes, along the way you may make bad choices. But these bad choices should not divert you from the path you have chosen. They are simply side trips on the road you are walking.

One way a low-carber can make it for the long haul is by doing *planned cheats*. Planned cheats may work differently for everyone—after all, you know your body best! Take a look at the following example, and maybe you can add it to your low-carb arsenal.

Essentially, how I handle a planned cheat is like a Carbohydrate Addicts Diet (CAD) Reward Meal. The meal begins with a small plate of salad. The rest of the meal is divided into thirds. One-third is meat, and one-third is a good low-carb veggie. The final element is some carby food, like a dinner roll or a dessert. The entire meal must be eaten within one hour.

I've found that planned cheats are useful in helping me to celebrate anniversaries and other special occasions when bringing my own food simply is not an option. Since I follow the Atkins diet, "benign dietary ketosis," (the measurable state of burning fat as outlined in Dr. Atkins's *New Diet Revolution*), is important for me. What I've found is that by allowing myself these reward meals, I can stay in ketosis if the timing and balance is correct. I have also found that I cannot do a planned cheat more than once every couple of weeks. It does spark cravings and weight gain if I do it more than that.

The second way to do a planned cheat is by simply going off the diet plan for a meal. For instance, my best friend and I love to go to this little Mexican restaurant every so often, so I simply plan that one meal to be off plan. I eat very low-carb the rest of the day and get right back on track the next. By employing similar strategies that work for you, you'll still enjoy family and friends without beating yourself up over blowing the diet. If you plan to cheat and return to your diet the following meal, there is nothing to beat yourself up over!

With that said, how do you make good choices while you are on the run, as so many of us are?

Be Aware of Where You Will Be Eating in Advance

If you're eating dinner at someone's home, try to find out what the menu is in advance. If they are planning something like lasagna, you can request they reserve some of the meat sauce and cheese for you without the noodles. It may feel awkward at first, but you'll find that most people are very understanding, especially as the low-carb way of life gains popularity. For example, when asking for low-carb variations, you can tell your host that the carbs don't make you feel well. Other folks are fond of saying, "I'm allergic to carbs; they make me break out in fat!" Usually, a gentle and/or humorous answer will help the host realize you are serious.

Of course, there will always be situations you can't change. If you find yourself in a situation where the host is unwilling or unable to change the menu to suit your dietary needs, you have a few choices:

1.   Eat before the function. Go with your tummy already satisfied and take very small portions of the meal to be polite, or simply abstain.

2. Bring your own food. I can't tell you how many times I've had to do this. A simple tossed salad and some leftover meat can really help you out.

3. Take that meal off. This is hard for some people, but some folks are extremely successful at just having the one meal of whatever they are served and getting right back on their food plan with the next meal. Just be aware, you may struggle with cravings for up to three days or much longer.

What If the Meal Is Unplanned, but Unavoidable?

Again, if you end up at someone's house for an impromptu dinner, you can use the strategies in the previous list. But no matter how much you plan, sometimes there just aren't any good choices.

Recently, I ended up spending an entire day at the hospital with a friend. The only place for me to eat was the hospital cafeteria, where there were no good choices for me. The best choice I could find was some chicken gravy and really pathetic broccoli. In situations like this, all you can do is your best. Just eat what there is, and get back on the program with the next meal.

What about Unforeseen Temptations?

Picture this: You're at the office, and one of your coworkers brings donuts in for a treat. You know you shouldn't have one because you need to stay on plan. What should you do?

There are always going to be times when you're tempted, but being prepared is half the battle. Try keeping packets of sunflower seeds or almonds in your desk or in your car for your weak moments.

Usually, by having almonds I am able to stay on plan even when folks are offering me cake and cookies. Frankly, I don't like the taste of those things anymore anyway. I would much rather eat real food!

Tips for Smart Salad Choices

When living the low-carb way, you'll quickly find that salads can be one of your best friends. However, there are plenty of pitfalls to avoid when it comes to making smart salad choices, especially when you're unable to make the salad for yourself.

First, let's talk dressings. A good rule of thumb is to avoid any of the red or pink dressings, like French, Thousand Island, or Russian. All of these dressings have a high sugar content. Better choices include white dressings like ranch, blue cheese (Roquefort), or Caesar. Usually, these dressings have little or no sugar, thus minimal carbs per serving. Another good choice would be lemon or vinegar and olive oil with salt and pepper.

Now, let's get on to the nuts and bolts of a good salad. When I say "salad" some folks still think of the salad bar standbys of macaroni and potato. Those certainly would not be appropriate for a low-carber to eat! If you're at a salad bar, there are lots of temptations, but if you're armed with the right knowledge, you'll still be able to make good choices.

Here are a few items that you should avoid when you're doing the salad thing:

- Croutons
- Noodles
- Syrupy canned fruits
- Raisins

- Grapes
- Bananas
- Large pieces of carrot (a few shreds are fine if you are past the induction stage of the Atkins diet)
- Three-bean salad
- Pickled beets
- Soup (most salad bar soups are thickened with flour or loaded with potatoes or noodles)

Here's a quickie list of great low-carb salad ingredients:

- Salad greens
- Spinach
- Broccoli
- Cauliflower
- Celery
- Snow peas (pea pods)
- Baby corn
- Green onions
- Mushrooms
- Eggs
- Cheese
- Meats (like smoked salmon and pepperoni)
- Sunflower kernels, etc.

Tomatoes, peppers, and cottage cheese are also acceptable choices. Just be sure to use them in small amounts. Generally, if it is sweet tasting, like beets and tomatoes, use it in extreme moderation, especially if you are just starting out on the low-carb way of life.

Snacking

Some folks are snackers; others aren't. While some folks almost never snack, others prefer to eat many small meals a day. Most folks seem to fall right in the middle of the snack spectrum: three meals and a snack or two during the day.

Reality check: The main purpose of snacking is to keep your blood sugar and insulin in balance. If you go too long between meals, even though you are low-carbing, you can still have a blood sugar crash. Snacking can help prevent that dreaded crash. But be sure to snack smart. Have snacks as often as you need without going overboard. As always, watch your own carb allowance when choosing your snacks. If you have a very low personal carb threshold, you certainly don't want to snack on higher-carb foods like those in the second list that follows. Instead, choose your snacks from the first list.

What is one supposed to snack on while they are low-carbing? Certainly not cupcakes and chips! There are plenty of smart snacking options that can keep you out of trouble. I've compiled some suggestions here to help you get started. This list is by no means comprehensive, but it should help get your own creative snacking juices flowing!

Snacks under 5 Grams of Carbs per Serving (ounce):
Snack tip: Premeasure snacks into plastic bags so there is little risk of overdoing it and making your snack into a meal.

Cheese
Hard-boiled eggs
Egg Salad (page 65), scooped with pork rinds or
   celery sticks

Macadamia nuts

Raw almonds

Sunflower seeds in the shell

Candied Almonds (page 186)

Orange Essence Almonds (page 197)

Ranch Almonds (page 198)

Sweet-and-Spicy Almonds, Take Two (page 207)

Roasted Pecans (page 199)

Savory Pecans (page 200)

Cooked chicken

Pork rinds (plain or flavored, but not barbecue!)

Garlic Cheese Dip (page 192), with pork rinds or celery for dipping

Simply Guacamole (page 204), with pork rinds or celery for dipping

Smoked Salmon Dip (page 205), with pork rinds or celery for dipping

Spinach Dip (page 206), with pork rinds or celery for dipping

Deli lunchmeat with cream cheese, sliced cheese, or a pickle rolled up in it

Sugar-free gelatin dessert

Celery stuffed with cream cheese, blue cheese, peanut butter, almond butter, etc.

Pepperoni slices with mozzarella cheese warmed in the microwave and served with Pizza Sauce (page 158) for dipping

Diet root beer with a bit of cream added to make a low-carb "float"

Cheeseburger (small) without bun and no ketchup

Raw veggies like broccoli, cauliflower, mushrooms

Zingy Pumpkin Kernels (page 210)

Snacks under 10 Grams of Carbs per Serving (ounce):
As with the previous items, you will want to measure
your snacks and be aware of how much you are eating.
You certainly don't want to "spoil your dinner"!

Rye cracker with almond butter, peanut butter, or Egg
    Salad (page 65)
Cranberry Muffins (page 39)
Party Wraps (page 153)
Berries with cream
Pumpkin Granola (page 48)
Cinnamon Tarts (page 188)
Elephant Ears (page 190)
Low-Carb Quesadillas (page 46)
Low-Carb Tortilla Chips (page 194) with Refried
    Soybeans (page 165)
Nutty Caramel Roll-Ups (page 196)
Piggies in Blankets (page 156)
German Chocolate Raspberry Yogurt (page 222)
Simply Delicious Yogurt Parfaits (page 231)
Vanilla Yogurt (page 234)
Yogurt Swirl Dessert (page 235)
Zucchini Nut Bread (page 211)

The Skinny on Protein Bars

With all of this snack talk, you're probably wondering why
I haven't listed the very popular low-carb meal replacement
bars and candies as a snacking option. As a moderator and
contributing writer at *LowCarbEating.com*, my colleagues and
I talk to countless people who come to our message forums
saying that they are having trouble losing, even though they
are "following the diet perfectly." When we ask to see their

menus, the majority of the time they include items such as low-carb meal replacement bars and candies. While these products *might be* suitable for some once they are near or have reached their goal weight, I would recommend the majority of low-carbers avoid these products. I have experienced weight gain, sometimes significant, from adding these bars and candies to my diet. I've also encountered many low-carbers on the message board who have the same story.

Here's the scoop: Those bars and candies are all loaded with "sugar alcohols." Sugar alcohols, like maltitol, can cause significant blood sugar spikes in many people, as I understand from my study. These snacks can cause many people's blood sugar to respond the same as it would with normal sugar, but have absolutely no effect on blood glucose levels in other people. That makes them very much a "your mileage may vary" kind of food. Unfortunately, most of us who need to follow the low-carb way of life for weight loss and insulin control are among the ones that these products have negative effects on. The one exception seems to be the new sugar alcohol erythritol. It doesn't seem to cause the dramatic rise in blood sugar or the intestinal troubles that the other sugar alcohols do. As always, proceed with caution and observe your own results well.

As all of the major low-carb plans agree, balancing blood glucose levels is the key to both weight loss and general health. Insulin spikes, which happen when blood sugar rises, are the culprits for a number of health problems. That is why I recommend that people, in general, avoid these products.

If you've been having problems losing weight and you're using the bars or candies, try taking a break from them for a week and see what happens. Once you have reached your goal weight and/or health goals, you can try to introduce these products into your way of eating. Observe your reaction to them. If they don't cause cravings, bloating, or weight gain over a period of time, they might be useful for you. As always, I recommend you eat "real" rather than highly processed foods.

Oh No! I've Got a Craving!

What can you do besides just cave in and eat that cupcake or packet of chips? Don't despair—there are many strategies to keep yourself "on the straight and narrow low-carb way." Here are my top ten craving busters:

1. Have a glass of water. I find that often when I have weird food cravings, I'm actually thirsty.

2. Eat some protein, like a piece of chicken or a boiled egg. One friend of mine uses a hard-boiled egg as her "guideline." Whenever she has a craving, or just thinks she's hungry at a weird time, she asks herself if she would like a boiled egg. If the answer is "no," then she isn't hungry and doesn't eat. If the answer is "yes," then she has the egg. By using this strategy, among others, as part of her low-carb food plan, my friend has not only lost, but has kept off over fifty pounds for over five years!

3. Rest. Sometimes a craving can actually mean you're fatigued. Is it time for a break? Sit down, put your feet in the air, and take a breather. Many times, just shifting your focus can beat the craving.

4. Remove yourself from the situation. Sometimes, that is the only way to really stay in control. If there is a box of candy on a coworker's desk, you may simply need to walk away. If you are eating dinner and an "offending" food is in front of you, move the food. I've often had to employ both of these tactics.

5.   Have some kefir or apple cider vinegar. Sometimes what our bodies need is a boost of nutrition. A glass of kefir, either plain or fixed as an Easy Kefir Smoothie (page 189) or a teaspoon of organic, unfiltered apple cider vinegar, either plain or mixed in water with a bit of SteviaPlus, will often knock cravings right on their keesters!

6.   Think about what you *can* have, rather than what you *can't*. A friend of mine recently had to drive by what had been one of his favorite restaurants, one that is inappropriate for this way of eating. Of course, a craving set in immediately. He said, "I yanked that train of thought off the tracks by focusing on the Oyster Bar that is right next door. I thought about how good the seafood is, and how I can have as much of it as I want. The urge for the unacceptable food disappeared."

7.   "Nothing tastes as good as thin feels." Many, many folks use that line as a defense mechanism when the cravings really hit! Next time you're hit with a craving, give it a try.

8.   Think about how good you feel now and how bad you'll feel later. Since a great many of us are actually sensitive to the foods we crave most, eating them will cause us to feel miserable afterward. Take donuts, for instance. They used to be one of my greatest weaknesses, but I know how badly I would feel after eating one, so I just won't go there!

9.   Get support. Call a friend if the cravings get too bad. Ask your friend to help you stay accountable. If you don't have anyone you can trust that way, then find an online community or even a weight loss support group and make yourself accountable there.

10. Keep a journal. I find the act of journaling helps me make better choices, especially since mine is a public one online!

Dealing with Friends and Family

Often, it is those closest to us that can cause us the greatest troubles in achieving our weight loss and health goals! While some folks are blessed with extremely supportive families and friends, others have friends and relatives that are actively against them achieving their goals.

I know one lady whose husband seems to actively seek out ways to defeat his wife's attempts at healthy eating. He stocks the pantry with macaroni and cheese and cupcakes after she's gone through and cleaned everything out and given all of the carby stuff away!

If you have to deal with issues like that, one way to cope is by giving the other members of your family a different section of the pantry or refrigerator for their "stuff." For instance, I find that if I keep the foods I shouldn't have on a bottom shelf, I'm not as likely to blow my food plan.

Whatever it takes, you have to take charge of what is in your home the place that has the potential to be either your greatest shelter or the greatest place of temptation.

Dining Out

Sure, eating out can be challenging, but with a little creative thinking, you can enjoy a meal out without any guilt or worry.

Mexican

If you avoid certain pitfalls, you can enjoy a great meal at a Mexican sit-down restaurant. Just follow these tips:

- Avoid the tortillas!
- Avoid the chips!

- Replace the standard side dishes of beans and rice with a salad.
- Get creative with your salad dressing options.

If your carb allowance is high enough, you may be able to have a few chips or a tortilla, just be very aware of what you're eating for the rest of the meal. As mentioned in the previous list, when you order your entrée, you can avoid the standard rice and beans side dishes by requesting that the kitchen replace them with a salad. Most restaurants will kindly oblige your request. When you eat at a Mexican restaurant, you have a unique option for salad dressings. Opt for salsa and sour cream or lemon/lime juice and oil for a tasty and inventive dressing variation.

For your main dish, be careful to choose one that is not breaded or wrapped in a tortilla. Different restaurants have different specialties, but most will have carnitas (pork), carne asada (beef steak), or some type of fish that is not breaded or wrapped. Also, many Mexican restaurants serve fajitas on a sizzling platter and provide tortillas on the side so you can wrap them yourself. Skip the tortillas, and you've got a great dinner! If you're feeling confused, don't be afraid to ask your server for assistance in choices. Most will be happy to guide you to the right part of the menu.

Italian
Even when you go to a traditional Italian restaurant, there are low-carb choices! They may not be abundant, but with a little creativity, you'll have no problems. For example, try dishes such as chicken or veal parmigiana (which have marinara sauce and cheese). Also, most Italian restaurants offer side dishes of meatballs or Italian sausage, so one option

would be to pair that with a salad on the side. Here are some Italian dining tips:

- Avoid the rolls or bread that are often served with the meal.
- If there is a sandwich menu, you can order a nice meat sandwich, and just skip the bread.
- If a main course is served over pasta, skip the pasta.
- Avoid the potatoes.
- As always, steer clear of dessert.

If you end up at a pizza place, then your challenge is slightly greater. However, many pizza establishments offer sandwich menus and salad. Just ask for the sandwich without the bread and have a salad on the side. If the restaurant doesn't offer those choices, try crustless pizza. Just eat the toppings off the pizza and leave the crust. Recently, many pizza restaurants have started to get into the low-carb way of eating. Ask your server if there are any low-carb menu choices. Just be aware that one person's definition of low- or lower-carb may not match yours. If all they've done is made a thin-crust pizza and called it "low-carb," this wouldn't be a wise meal choice.

Asian

Most Asian restaurants (Chinese, Thai, Japanese,) give choices of stir-fried veggies and meats. Skip anything that says it has noodles or rice in it. Even restaurants that specialize in the "noodle bowls" that are so popular will stir-fry some veggies and meat for you, unless it is a vegetarian restaurant! Remember—stir-fry is your friend.

Here's a quick list of tips for ordering Asian cuisine:

- Tell your server to "skip the gravy." This will help you to eliminate any high-carb sauces that come with your meal.
- Avoid rice and noodles.
- Specify "no sugar" when you ask about seasonings.
- The best seasonings to choose when ordering are garlic, ginger, herbs, and soy sauce.
- Avoid imitation crabmeat. (It's highly processed and loaded with sugar.)
- Avoid rice rolls and wraps.

Mongolian barbecue restaurants can either be a low-carber's bane or delight. Skip the "specialty" sauces with fancy names like Mongolian and hoisin; almost all of them have sugar in them. When in doubt, just put a tiny drop of the sauce onto the edge of your bowl and taste it. You'll know if it has sugar in it. If you know your options and choose accordingly, you can enjoy a very delightful Asian meal.

Steak Houses

This is one of the easiest places to make good choices. As always, be sure to avoid the bread and potatoes. If they offer a veggie, make sure you ask what it is. As long as it isn't peas, corn, or "mixed veggies," you often can ask for double veggies or extra salad instead of the potato. Some steak houses even offer cottage cheese instead of potatoes. (This applies to other categories as well, but is most common in steak houses.) You can get grilled onions or mushrooms for your steak and have a really nice dinner.

Seafood

My favorite seafood restaurant, McGrath's, offers a wide choice of grilled and smoked fish. Unfortunately, this isn't typical for all seafood restaurants. Many limit their menus to battered fish and coleslaw. Again, make the best choices you can, and, of course, the general guidelines of skipping bread and pasta apply.

Other Ethnic Establishments

There are so many choices out there now, especially if you live in or near a large metropolitan area. My suggestion would be to speak with your server. Tell the waiter you want meat and veggies without sugar or flour and see what he suggests. Most menus describe the food available and most servers are happy to help; after all, that is how they earn their tips! Nevertheless, following are a few suggestions.

Greek

Certain Greek foods are great options for low-carbers, especially if you stick with the grilled meats, such as beef, lamb, or chicken. Kebabs are a terrific choice. Just be sure to ask your server to skip the bread. Greek salads are also a great choice for a low-carber—pile it high with plenty of lettuce, Greek olives, Feta cheese, onions, and hot peppers! You can also order a gyro (pronounced "hee-RO") built as a salad. Just ask them to keep the bread.

Japanese

Sushi restaurants are full of good choices for you. Now, before you stop reading right here, not all sushi is raw fish! In fact, "sushi" actually refers to the type of rice used in this popular dish. Of course, that should raise red flags right there. Instead, opt for "sashimi," which is just the fish—and yes, it is raw. Seaweed salads and many Japanese soups are also good choices. If you're ordering a cooked entrée, there are lots of meat and vegetable choices for you. You can simply ask your server to use sauces without sugar and skip the rice and other high-carb fare.

Fast Food

It seems like we are a nation of people always eating on the run. What happens when fast food meets the low-carber? Or, should I say, when the low-carber meets fast food? Here are some tips to help you survive the encounter.

Mexican

This is a tough one, as everything is either breaded or wrapped in a tortilla. The smartest low-carb choice is to get a taco salad and simply not eat the tortilla shell it comes in. While simply eating the fillings out of a taco is also an option, beware! Most of the national chains add a significant amount of white flour to their taco meat. Unless you're really between a rock and a hard place, try to avoid Mexican fast-food restaurants.

Sub Shops and Delis

This would include Subway and restaurants like Arby's, as well as "mom-and-pop" establishments and grocery delicatessens. While sub shops might seem like a great option at first, look closely. They generally use highly processed lunchmeats, which contain nitrates; these are known carcinogens. If this is your only choice, though, most of these establishments now offer salads with meat toppings. If all else fails, you can order a large sandwich and skip the bread.

Recently, many chains have started offering low-carb friendly wraps and sandwiches. Of the national chains, Blimpie is by far my favorite. They weigh the meat for each sandwich individually, and they use very fresh ingredients. If you have to eat at this type of restaurant, you might check on the availability of a low-carb menu.

Delis offer a few fine options for low-carbers, such as sausages (if they aren't swimming in barbecue sauce), and roasted or rotisserie chicken. Be sure to avoid any prepared salads like potato and coleslaw, which are loaded with sugar; instead, choose a side salad.

Asian Fast Food

This would include the "Quick Wok"–type establishments as well as buffets. This is a difficult place to make good choices. For the most part, the food is precooked and covered with sauce before it is put out. On the rare occasion that they do make the food fresh, follow the guidelines for dining in Asian restaurants (see page 16). More likely, you will just have to make the best choices from the foods offered. Especially avoid the breaded and wrapped food and red sauces. Instead, opt for the stir-fried dishes and avoid the noodles and as much of the sauce as possible. Some places may offer a "healthy choice" option that consists of steamed veggies and chicken or shrimp, so go for that, if it is available.

Burger Places

Most of the national chains, including McDonald's, Burger King, and Wendy's, now offer a salad menu. Ranch dressing is probably your safest choice when ordering fast-food salad. Other dressings can be full of sugar. If you're dying for a burger, there are plenty of choices. For example, you can order a bacon cheeseburger, just throw away the bun, and have a side salad. Actually, most of the national chains offer low-carb plates for their diners. You will want to avoid the breaded meat patties and sweetened sauces like ketchup, sweet pickle relish, barbecue, and Thousand Island–type burger sauces.

Chicken Places

Again, this could be a tough choice. Many of the chains now offer roasted or rotisserie chicken, so choose that instead of anything breaded. If you're stuck with breaded chicken, just peel as much of the breading off as you can. As always, be sure to avoid the potatoes and coleslaw and opt for the dependable side salad. Check out the veggie offerings at these places as well—green beans or broccoli can be good choices for a low-carber. A word of caution: Several national chains are advertising their products as "low-carb," when they are simply the same items they have been selling all along. As always, "let the buyer beware!"

Fish and Chips

Most fish and chip places are offering better options these days. Many of them are paying more attention to those trying to eat in a more healthful manner. Avoid the breaded fish, coleslaw, and fries; request grilled fish and a side salad. Some national chains now have several grilled items on their menus, and you can substitute the fries and coleslaw for a veggie and a salad. Often, these substitutions cost a little more, but for a better meal, it is worth it.

Breakfast Places

There are a number of restaurants that specialize in serving breakfast. In fact, some are so "into" breakfast that they serve it all day! How is a good low-carber to survive at a place that is trying to fill you full of pancakes, waffles, and French toast? Remember one very important low-carb breakfast rule: Omelettes are your friend! They are usually large enough on their own to satisfy you without the addition of the potatoes, toast, and flapjacks. For a yummy omelette at home, try the Clubhouse Omelette (page 37) and Clubhouse Sauce (page 63). If you're out for breakfast, order the omelette of your choice and ask for some extra veggies on the side.

You don't have to have just an omelette if you go out for breakfast, though. Many places offer steak and eggs, and pork chops. Even the old standby, bacon and eggs, is a great choice. Ask if you can have a side veggie, like grilled onions and mushrooms or some broccoli, and you won't feel like you are missing out on anything.

One Final Note

As time goes by, the low-carbohydrate way of living is becoming more and more common among the general population. More and more research is being done that shows this way of eating is an extremely healthy choice for a larger band of the populace than was ever previously thought by the medical community. More and more positive press and publicity is being given to carbohydrate-restricted diets. With all this, more restaurants are joining in! Keep your eye out for the many eating establishments that now offer "low-carb menus" to their guests.

Be aware, though, that most of these menus were not developed by practicing low-carb dieters. Many are there just to meet a perceived need. That said, go in with your eyes open. While a restaurant may have a low-carb menu, it may or may not be your best dining choice.

For example, I was recently at a restaurant that offered low-carb fare. It was austere! It was a plate of meat, cottage cheese, and a very small lettuce-only salad. Where were the veggies?

I chose otherwise, and I spoke with the manager afterward. I gave her some suggestions on how to improve the restaurant's menu. She was truly thankful.

It is all about education. Once you have educated yourself, go and teach others.

How we start our day has a big impact on how our day will go. Be sure to eat a good breakfast!

Breakfasts

1

BACON AND THREE-CHEESE MINI-PIZZAS

Makes 4 servings

These handy little pizzas are a quick and easy make-ahead meal that you can serve to the whole gang. They also make a good lunch or supper dish with a side salad. Either way, they are delicious.

½ pound bacon, cut into ½" strips
½ sweet onion, chopped (about ¼ cup)
¼ teaspoon dried marjoram
½ teaspoon dried parsley flakes
1 cup cottage cheese
2 eggs
¼ cup grated Parmesan cheese
¼ teaspoon lemon pepper
Cooking oil spray
4 (6") low-carb tortillas
1 cup shredded cheese (Monterey jack, Colby, Cheddar, or a blend)
½ teaspoon dried basil
Simply Guacamole (page 204), optional

1. Cook the bacon in a medium-sized frying pan over medium heat until it just begins to soften, about 3 to 4 minutes. Add the onion, marjoram, and parsley; cook, stirring often, for about 10 to 12 minutes or until the onion is just becoming golden brown. The bacon should be brown and fully cooked, but not crisp.
2. Meanwhile, stir together the cottage cheese, eggs, Parmesan, and lemon pepper.
3. Spray four 8" to 9" pie pans or a very large baking sheet with cooking oil spray.
4. Place the tortillas into the pans. If using a baking sheet, place them so that the edges of the tortillas are not touching. Divide the cheese mixture evenly between the tortillas, leaving at least ½" around the edges uncovered.

5. Using a slotted spoon, divide the bacon and onions atop the cheese mixture. Sprinkle an even amount of the shredded cheese over the bacon on each of the pizzas. Sprinkle each with basil.
6. Bake them at 375°F for about 10 to 12 minutes, or until the filling is set and the cheese is melted. Cut the pizzas into fourths and top with guacamole, if desired.

Nutritional information per serving
(not including the guacamole):
Carbohydrates: 16 grams; Effective Carb Count: 7 grams;
Protein: 35 grams; Fat: 35 grams; Calories: 499

Reduced-Fat Variation:
Use turkey bacon, fat-free cottage cheese, and reduced-fat cheese.
Follow all other instructions as given.
Carbohydrates: 17 grams; Effective Carb Count: 8 grams;
Protein: 33 grams; Fat: 20 grams; Calories: 360

BASIC SCRAMBLED EGGS

Makes 1 serving

When I was thinking of recipes for this book, a friend suggested this recipe to me. It is something I make without even thinking about it, but she pointed out that not everyone can make eggs that taste good. Now they can!

2 large eggs
¼ teaspoon seasoning salt
1–2 teaspoons coconut oil or lard

1. Beat the eggs and seasoning salt in a small bowl with a fork until they are frothy.
2. Place the coconut oil into a small frying pan over medium heat. When the oil has melted, add the eggs to the pan. Allow them to cook, without stirring, until the bottom begins to set. Don't let the eggs brown.
3. Flip the eggs over and cook them until they are just solid, moving them around and breaking them up slightly in the pan until the wetness disappears. Serve them immediately.

Nutritional information per serving
(figured using 1½ teaspoons coconut oil):
Carbohydrates: 1 gram; Effective Carb Count: 1 gram;
Protein: 11 grams; Fat: 16 grams; Calories: 191

Reduced-Fat Variation:
Use cooking oil spray instead of the coconut oil.
Follow all other instructions as given.
Carbohydrates: 1 gram; Effective Carb Count: 1 gram;
Protein: 11 grams; Fat: 9 grams; Calories: 132

BEST BACON

Makes about 12 to 24 servings

Cooking bacon is time-consuming and messy! If you use this method, you will have much less mess, and you can cook it up in larger quantities for use later.

1–2 pounds bacon, cured without sugar and nitrates, if available

1. Lay out the bacon evenly on a large baking sheet. Be sure the edges don't overlap. (All the bacon may not fit on the baking sheet at first. The bacon will shrink as it cooks, leaving more room. The additional slices may be added at that time.)
2. Place the baking sheet into a 350°F oven for approximately 30 minutes. Remove the bacon from the pan when the fatty portion is translucent; it should no longer be white. (It won't appear brown the way pan-fried bacon does, instead the meat will be a deep red color. If it is overcooked, it will crumble when cooled. If it is perfect, it will be tender and juicy.) One of the benefits of cooking the bacon this way is that it will lay flat rather than curling up as pan-fried bacon does. Place on a serving plate lined with paper towels to drain.

Nutritional information per serving:
Carbohydrates: trace; Effective Carb Count: trace;
Protein: 11 grams; Fat: 19 grams; Calories: 218

Reduced-Fat Variation:
Use turkey bacon and follow all instructions as given.
Carbohydrates: 1 gram; Effective Carb Count: 1 gram;
Protein: 6 grams; Fat: 7 grams; Calories: 92

BREAKFAST BURRITOS

Makes 8 servings

This is a staple at my house. I think it is one of my kids' favorite breakfasts! These can also be a part of your "low-carb game plan" of being prepared in advance for unexpected meals out. Grab one or two from the freezer and take them along with you. You won't feel deprived, and you will be well fed while everyone else around you is eating coffee and donuts!

8 (6") low-carb tortillas
8 slices (4 ounces) Monterey jack or Colby cheese
8 slices cooked bacon or 8 links cooked sausage
8 eggs
Seasoning salt, to taste
Coconut oil or lard, for frying
Salsa (optional)
Sour cream (optional)
Chives (optional)

1. Heat a large skillet over medium heat and place the tortillas into the skillet one at a time, warming them on each side for about 30 to 45 seconds. Remove to plates. Place the cheese and bacon down the center of each tortilla.
2. Meanwhile, combine the eggs and seasoning salt in a small bowl, mixing them until they are slightly frothy. Melt the fat in a medium-sized skillet over medium heat. Pour the eggs into the skillet and allow them to cook, without stirring, until the bottom becomes opaque and solid enough to flip, about 1½ minutes. Turn the eggs over and cook them until they are set.
3. Cut the egg into 8 equal pieces and place one piece onto each tortilla. Fold the tortillas up at the bottom and then over on each side. Serve the optional ingredients at the table, if desired.

4. To freeze for later use, individually wrap each burrito in waxed paper, then place them in a sealable freezer bag. (They warm best in the microwave if you let them stand overnight in the fridge, but they can be reheated directly from the freezer.)
5. To reheat the burritos, wrap each burrito in a paper towel and heat in the microwave for 1 to 2 minutes, turning each about halfway through.

Nutritional information per serving:
Carbohydrates: 13 grams; Effective Carb Count: 4 grams;
Protein: 19 grams; Fat: 21 grams; Calories: 297

Reduced-Fat Variation:
Use turkey bacon, reduced-fat cheese, and cooking spray
instead of coconut oil, and follow the instructions given.
Carbohydrates: 13 grams; Effective Carb Count: 4 grams;
Protein: 20 grams; Fat: 11 grams; Calories: 209

BREAKFAST BURRITOS
WITH CHORIZO AND EGGS

Makes 8 servings

This is an easy make-ahead meal. Keep them in the freezer for those mornings when all you have time for is something zapped in the microwave. For a real treat, add a sprinkling of cheese to the burrito before sealing it.

1 recipe Chorizo and Eggs (page 36)
8 (6") low-carb tortillas
Water

1. Prepare the Chorizo and Eggs (page 36).
2. Heat a large skillet on medium and place the tortillas in the skillet one at a time, warming them on each side for about 30 seconds. Alternatively, you may warm the tortillas in the microwave for about 20 seconds each.
3. Put some water in a small dish. Place a warmed tortilla on a clean work surface. Place ⅛ of the filling (about ½ cup) down the center of the tortilla, leaving at least an inch on each end. Fold up the ends and then fold over one long side of the burrito. Dip your finger into the water and slightly dampen the edges of the remaining unfolded side of the tortilla. Fold it over the burrito and press it to seal. Repeat with the remaining tortillas.
4. Place the finished burritos, folded-side down, onto a baking sheet and place them into the freezer until they are frozen solid. Remove them from the freezer and place them into freezer bags.
5. To reheat: Wrap a burrito with a paper towel and microwave it on medium power until it is hot, about 2 minutes. Alternatively, you may partially reheat it in the microwave, then pan-fry it in a bit of cooking fat until it is golden brown.

Nutritional information per serving:
Carbohydrates: 13 grams; Effective Carb Count: 4 grams;
Protein: 12 grams; Fat: 8 grams; Calories: 144

BUBBY'S BUTTERMILK FLAPJACKS

Makes about 20 pancakes

My son had been begging for pancakes for weeks. One morning, I was inspired to make him some, and this was the result. They are delicious served hot, or you can individually freeze them, then reheat them in the microwave. You can even roll cooked sausage links in them and have them as a meal on the go! This makes a really great special meal with Decadent French Toast Topping (page 41) or you can use them as a "breakfast for dinner" meal with eggs, sausage, and Cauliflower Hash Browns (page 79) on the side.

Dry ingredients:
1 cup vital wheat gluten flour
1 cup ground almonds
1¼ teaspoons baking soda
¾ teaspoon baking powder
1 teaspoon sea salt
2 packets sucralose

Wet ingredients:
2 eggs
2 cups kefir or buttermilk
¼ cup butter, melted
½ cup blueberries
Coconut oil or cooking oil spray, for frying

1. Combine the dry ingredients in a large mixing bowl; set them aside.
2. In a smaller bowl, combine the wet ingredients except the oil, mixing them well. Pour the wet ingredients into the dry ingredients and stir them until they are just combined. If the batter is too thick, you may need to add some water to make it thinner.
3. Cook the pancakes on a medium-hot griddle or frying pan that has been lightly greased with coconut oil or cooking oil spray. Cook the pancakes on one side until bubbles cover the surface and the edges have just set; flip the pancakes and cook them

until they are golden brown. (It is likely that you will need to decrease the temperature of your griddle as you go, ending up on medium-low heat for most of the pancakes.) Continue to add grease as needed to the pan to prevent sticking.

Nutritional information per serving (1 pancake):
Carbohydrates: 3 grams; Effective Carb Count: 2 grams;
Protein: 13 grams; Fat: 8 grams; Calories: 130

Reduced-Fat Variation:
Use reduced-fat buttermilk and follow the instructions as given.
Carbohydrates: 4 grams; Effective Carb Count: 3 grams;
Protein: 13 grams; Fat: 7 grams; Calories: 125

CHEESY HAM AND EGGS

Makes 6 servings

I often make these eggs for Sunday breakfast because I feel like I'm making something special, but it doesn't take an hour. Use the leftovers and make breakfast burritos out of them, following the instructions for Breakfast Burritos with Chorizo and Eggs (page 32).

12 eggs
1 teaspoon seasoning salt
1 tablespoon coconut oil or lard
⅓ pound deli ham, chicken, or turkey, diced
1 cup shredded cheese (Colby, Cheddar, Monterey jack, or a blend)

1. In a large bowl, beat the eggs with the seasoning salt until they are frothy. Do not dump the salt into the eggs all in one spot, but be sure and sprinkle it over their surface. If you dump it, you'll end up with all the salt all in one place!
2. Melt the coconut oil in a large frying pan over medium heat. Pour the eggs into the pan and cook them, stirring occasionally, until they are almost set. Add the meat and continue to cook the meat and eggs until the meat is heated through and the eggs are just set, about 1 minute.
3. Meanwhile, have a serving dish ready. Put about ⅓ of the cheese in the bottom of the dish. When the eggs are done, put ½ of the eggs into the bowl. Sprinkle with another ⅓ of the cheese and put the rest of the eggs on top of the cheese. Finally, sprinkle the eggs with the remaining cheese and cover the dish for a minute or so to let the cheese melt. Serve hot.

Nutritional information per serving:
Carbohydrates: 2 grams; Effective Carb Count: 2 grams;
Protein: 21 grams; Fat: 19 grams; Calories: 260

Reduced-Fat Variation:
Use low-fat versions of the meats and cheese and use cooking oil spray instead of the coconut oil. Follow all other remaining instructions as given.
Carbohydrates: 2 grams; Effective Carb Count: 2 grams;
Protein: 20 grams; Fat: 10 grams; Calories: 187

Q

CHORIZO AND EGGS

Makes 4 servings

When I was in college, I was friends with a Hispanic family. This was a favorite breakfast! This recipe is an integral part of Breakfast Burritos with Chorizo and Eggs (page 32), but it is just as delicious on its own. Serve this with Simply Guacamole (page 204), sour cream, and warmed tortillas for a real treat!

7–8 ounces Chorizo sausage
8 eggs

1. To remove the casing from the sausage, cut a hole in one end of it. Squeeze the sausage out into a medium-sized frying pan. Cook it over medium heat, breaking up the sausage as it cooks. Stir it frequently to prevent it from sticking to the pan.
2. Meanwhile, beat the eggs with a fork until they are frothy. When the sausage is quite bubbly, pour the eggs over the sausage; cook them, stirring occasionally, until they are just set, about 5 minutes.

Nutritional information per serving:
Carbohydrates: 1 gram; Effective Carb Count: 1 gram;
Protein: 13 grams; Fat: 12 grams; Calories: 165

CLUBHOUSE OMELETTE

Makes 1 large or 2 smaller servings

I had this omelette for the first time at a small restaurant in Seattle. While on that same trip, we ate at another restaurant with a very austere "low-carb" menu. The choices consisted of meat, cottage cheese, and a small side salad. I spoke with the manager, suggesting another veggie choice be added, and perhaps a larger salad. They have made the changes I suggested. All you have to do is speak up—you never know what might come from it!'

3 large eggs
¼ teaspoon seasoning salt
½ tablespoon coconut oil or lard

Filling:
½ cup shredded cheese (Monterey jack, Colby, Cheddar, or a blend)
6 pepperoni slices (about 1 ounce)
¼ cup diced chicken, cooked
2 ounces bulk pork sausage, cooked (about ½ cup)

Topping:
1 tablespoon shredded cheese
2 tablespoons Clubhouse Sauce (page 63)
2 tablespoons sliced olives
2 tablespoons diced tomatoes (optional)

1. Beat the eggs with the seasoning salt in a small bowl until they are frothy. Heat the oil in a medium-sized frying pan over medium heat until it just melts. Pour the eggs into the pan and cook them until they are nearly set, lifting the edges and allowing the uncooked egg to run into the bottom of the pan. When the eggs are nearly set, turn off the heat.
2. Layer the filling ingredients on one half of the omelette, in the order they are listed. Fold the other half of the omelette over the filling. Cut the omelette down the center, and slide it onto two plates.

3. Sprinkle the top of the omelette with the remaining cheese and drizzle the sauce over the top. Garnish with the olives and tomatoes.

Nutritional information per serving (2 servings):
Carbohydrates: 3 grams; Effective Carb Count: 3 grams; Protein: 27 grams; Fat: 41 grams; Calories: 490

Reduced-Fat Variation:
Use cooking oil spray instead of the coconut oil, and use reduced-fat cheese. Prepare the reduced-fat version of the Clubhouse Sauce (page 63). Follow all other instructions as given.
Carbohydrates: 3 grams; Effective Carb Count: 3 grams; Protein: 26 grams; Fat: 25 grams; Calories: 348

CRANBERRY MUFFINS

Makes 12 muffins

Serve these muffins to guests and they'll never know they are being given "health food"! If you have access to the preground almonds, I recommend using them. While it is easy enough to grind your own with a food processor, the preground ones make these little babies taste just like a whole-grain muffin. It is worth the extra expense for the end result. You can substitute the cranberries with whole blueberries for a really yummy variation. If you use ground blanched almonds, you will want to omit the water in the recipe.

Dry ingredients:
1¾ cups ground almonds
¼ cup vital wheat gluten flour
¼ cup soy protein isolate
½ teaspoon SteviaPlus
6 packets sucralose
1 tablespoon baking powder
½ teaspoon baking soda
½ teaspoon sea salt
½ teaspoon ground cinnamon
¼ teaspoon ground ginger
½ cup pecan pieces, broken

Wet ingredients:
¾ cup buttermilk or kefir
¼ cup water
½ teaspoon orange extract
½ cup whole cranberries
2 eggs
¼ cup olive oil
Cooking oil spray

1. Preheat the oven to 400°F. Combine the dry ingredients in a mixing bowl. In another bowl, combine all the wet ingredients except the cooking oil spray.
2. Stir the wet ingredients into the dry ingredients until they are just combined.
3. Spray a muffin pan with cooking oil spray. Divide the batter evenly between the muffin cups. If there are any without batter, put a little bit of water into the cups to prevent the pan from scorching and to help keep the muffins from drying out.
4. Bake them for 15 to 20 minutes or until the tops are golden.
5. When the muffins are done, slide a knife around the edges of each muffin to release them from the pan. Cool them on a rack. Store them in a plastic bag at room temperature for up to 2 days, or in the freezer for up to 1 month.

Nutritional information per serving:
Carbohydrates: 6 grams; Effective Carb Count: 4 grams;
Protein: 13 grams; Fat: 19 grams; Calories: 234

Reduced-Fat Variation:
Use applesauce instead of the olive oil and omit the water.
Follow all the remaining instructions as given.
Carbohydrates: 7 grams; Effective Carb Count: 5 grams;
Protein: 13 grams; Fat: 14 grams; Calories: 198

DECADENT FRENCH TOAST TOPPING

Makes 8 servings

This stuff is just amazing. It is so simple to make, and always gets rave reviews! Serve over French Toast, Low-Carbed (page 43) or Bubby's Buttermilk Flapjacks (page 33).

> ½ cup sliced fresh or frozen (thawed with juices) strawberries
> 1 cup yogurt
> ½ teaspoon vanilla extract
> ½ teaspoon SteviaPlus
> 2 tablespoons sugar-free maple syrup
> ½ cup cream
> 2 packets sucralose

1. In a mixing bowl, combine the strawberries and their juices, the yogurt, vanilla, SteviaPlus, and maple syrup. Mix it well, breaking up the strawberries so their juices work their way through the sauce.
2. In another mixing bowl, whip the cream with an electric mixer until peaks form. Add the sucralose, and continue mixing until combined.
3. Combine the whipped cream with the yogurt mixture. Mix it until it is just combined. Do not overmix the topping—otherwise you will end up with a runny mess!

Nutritional information per serving:
Carbohydrates: 2 grams; Effective Carb Count: 2 grams; Protein: 1 gram; Fat: 5 grams; Calories: 59

FLAX CEREAL

Yields 6 cups, which makes 16 servings

Flax is one of those amazing "superfoods." It is a veritable powerhouse of essential fatty acids, dietary fiber, vitamins, and minerals. While you are enjoying this yummy cereal, you can take comfort in the fact that you are also doing something really great for your body!

4 cups ground flaxseeds (3 cups whole seeds)
2 cups milk and egg protein powder
2 teaspoons ground cinnamon
½ teaspoon sea salt
4 teaspoons SteviaPlus
12 packets sucralose
butter or cream (optional)

To mix the cereal (2 servings):
¾ cup mix
1¼ cups water
¼ teaspoon extract of your choice (chocolate, maple, vanilla, etc.)

1. If you are grinding your own seeds, place about ⅓ to ½ cup seeds in a blender container and pulverize them on medium-high speed. (I prefer to leave some of the seeds unbroken. This gives the cereal a multigrain feel in the mouth. If you prefer a creamier cereal, pulverize the seeds completely.) Repeat this process for all of the remaining seeds. Please note: A food processor will not work for this recipe, as the seeds just spin around the blade and don't grind. A blender is necessary to grind the seeds.
2. Combine all of the ingredients in a large bowl or gallon-size zipper-sealed plastic bag. Mix the cereal very well and store in a covered container (or the bag) in the refrigerator.
3. To prepare the cereal: Combine the ingredients as listed above and stir this mixture until it is smooth. Microwave the cereal on high for 2 to 3 minutes or until it is hot and somewhat foamy across the top. Add butter or cream as desired.

Nutritional information per serving:
Carbohydrates: 11 grams; Effective Carb Count: 3 grams;
Protein: 15 grams; Fat: 10 grams; Calories: 181

FRENCH TOAST, LOW-CARBED

Makes 8 servings

Enjoy this delicious breakfast treat spread with peanut or almond butter, if you like. Top it with a generous dollop of Decadent French Toast Topping (page 41), and finish it off with a drizzling of sugar-free maple syrup. You can double or even triple this recipe and freeze the extras for superquick and easy breakfasts!

4 eggs
⅛ teaspoon sea salt
½ teaspoon Sweet & Slender
½ teaspoon ground cinnamon
½ teaspoon vanilla extract
½ cup kefir, buttermilk, or cream
8 slices low-carb bread, frozen
Lard or cooking oil spray, for frying

1. In a shallow dish, combine all of the ingredients *except* the bread and cooking fat. Mix them well with a fork or whisk. Dip the bread into the egg mixture, one slice at a time. Fry it on a hot griddle until it is golden on each side, about 5 minutes total.
2. Freeze any leftovers in freezer bags. To reheat, simply toast in the toaster until hot, and serve.

Nutritional information per serving:
Carbohydrates: 5 grams; Effective Carb Count: 5 grams;
Protein: 6 grams; Fat: 3 grams; Calories: 75

HEARTY BACON AND EGGS

Serves 6

You can serve this to a crowd or use the leftovers as a filling for breakfast burritos using the directions in Breakfast Burritos with Chorizo and Eggs (page 32). Have this first thing in the morning and you won't get the "hungries" later! Note: I used a brand of tortillas that has 9 total carbs and an ECC of 3 carbs per tortilla. If yours are different, then you will need to adjust the nutritional figures accordingly.

½ pound bacon, cut into ½" pieces
1 medium-sized onion, chopped
3 cloves garlic, minced (about 1½ tablespoons)
½ teaspoon lemon pepper
12 eggs
¼ teaspoon seasoning salt
1 tablespoon buttermilk
½ cup shredded cheese (Monterey jack, Colby, Cheddar, or a blend)
6 (6") low-carb tortillas (optional)
Simply Guacamole (page 204), optional

1. Cook the bacon in a large frying pan over medium heat until it is soft. Add the onion, garlic, and lemon pepper. Continue to cook them until they are just golden, about 10 minutes.
2. Drain off some of the excess fat, reserving part of it for cooking the eggs.
3. While the bacon and veggies are cooking, combine the eggs, seasoning salt, and buttermilk in a large bowl. Beat them until they are well mixed and frothy.
4. Pour the eggs over the bacon mixture in the pan. Cook them until they are just set, about 8 minutes, stirring frequently.
5. Transfer the bacon and eggs to a serving dish and garnish with the cheese. Serve them with tortillas and guacamole at the table, if desired.

Nutritional information per serving:
Carbohydrates: 4 grams; Effective Carb Count: 4 grams;
Protein: 25 grams; Fat: 30 grams; Calories: 396

Reduced-Fat Variation:
Use turkey bacon and reduced-fat cheese.
Follow all remaining instructions as given.
Carbohydrates: 4 grams; Effective Carb Count: 4 grams;
Protein: 19 grams; Fat: 17 grams; Calories: 251

Q

LOW-CARB QUESADILLAS

Makes 1 large or 2 small servings

I don't know anyone who doesn't like a quesadilla that has been properly prepared. We eat these at my house for breakfast, lunch, and dinner. Quesadillas are a simple staple that are part of my low-carb arsenal! Watch out, though. If you are still in weight loss mode, you *may* need to limit your low-carb tortillas and bread to once or twice a week.

1½ teaspoons coconut oil or lard
2 (6") low-carb tortillas
2 ounces cooked meat (chicken or pork), cut up
2–3 ounces cheese (Colby, Monterey jack, or a blend), shredded

1. Melt the oil in a large frying pan over medium heat. Place 1 of the tortillas into the pan. Layer it with half of the cheese, the meat, and the other half of the cheese. Place the remaining tortilla on top.
2. Cook the bottom layer until the tortilla begins to turn golden brown and the cheese has mostly melted. Carefully flip the tortilla and brown the other side. The total cooking time will be about 5 minutes.
3. To serve, cut the quesadilla into quarters with heavy-duty kitchen scissors (preferred) or a large knife. Serve hot.

**Nutritional information per serving
(2, with 3 ounces of cheese):**
Carbohydrates: 12 grams; Effective Carb Count: 3 grams;
Protein: 19 grams; Fat: 19 grams; Calories: 270

Reduced-Fat Variation:
Use chicken breast for the meat, reduced-fat cheese, and cooking oil spray instead of the lard. Follow the remaining instructions as given.
Carbohydrates: 13 grams; Effective Carb Count: 4 grams;
Protein: 21 grams; Fat: 5 grams; Calories: 159

PEPPERONI PIZZA OMELETTE

Makes 2 servings

This makes a great substantial breakfast or a terrific quick and easy dinner! Serve it with a salad and you've got a great meal.

3 large eggs
¼ teaspoon seasoning salt
½ tablespoon coconut oil or lard
2 tablespoons Pizza Sauce (page 158), or commercially prepared pizza sauce (but watch the carb counts!)
½ cup shredded mozzarella cheese
6 slices pepperoni (about 1 ounce)
¼ cup shredded Colby jack cheese
⅛ teaspoon Italian seasoning

1. Beat the eggs with the seasoning salt in a small bowl until they are frothy. Heat the oil in a medium-sized frying pan over medium heat until it just melts. Pour the eggs into the pan and cook them until they are nearly set, lifting the edges and allowing the uncooked egg to run into the bottom of the pan.
2. When the eggs are nearly set, turn off the heat. Spread the pizza sauce onto half of the omelette. Sprinkle half of the mozzarella cheese over the sauce, then place the pepperoni evenly over the cheese. Top the pepperoni with the remaining mozzarella.
3. Fold the empty side of the omelette over the filled side. Sprinkle the Colby jack cheese and the Italian seasoning over the omelette. Cover the pan and allow the cheeses to melt. Serve hot.

Nutritional information per serving:
Carbohydrates: 4 grams; Effective Carb Count: 4 grams;
Protein: 21 grams; Fat: 29 grams; Calories: 361

Reduced-Fat Variation:
Use cooking oil spray instead of the coconut oil and use reduced-fat cheese. Follow all the remaining instructions as given.
Carbohydrates: 4 grams; Effective Carb Count: 4 grams;
Protein: 23 grams; Fat: 20 grams; Calories: 289

PUMPKIN GRANOLA

Makes 12 servings

This is a terrific make-ahead breakfast food. It also comes in handy as a snack or topping for yogurt. Not to mention that it makes the whole house smell wonderful while it is baking!

4 cups coarsely chopped almonds
½ cup whole flaxseeds
½ cup unsweetened coconut
¼ cup soy protein isolate
½ cup milk and egg protein powder
2 teaspoons SteviaPlus
2 teaspoons ground ginger
2 teaspoons grated orange rind (zest)
2 teaspoons ground nutmeg
1 tablespoon ground cinnamon
½ teaspoon ground cloves
16 packets sucralose
¼ teaspoon sea salt
1½ cups pumpkin
2 teaspoons vanilla extract
2 cups Roasted Pecans (page 199)

1. In a large mixing bowl, combine the dry granola ingredients, then stir in the pumpkin and vanilla. Mix it until the pumpkin is evenly distributed throughout—the mixture will be very stiff. Stir in the Roasted Pecans (page 199), mixing well to incorporate them into the rest of the granola.
2. Spread the mixture on a large baking sheet and bake it at 325°F for about 25 minutes, stirring about halfway through. The granola should be golden brown and crunchy when done.
3. Let the granola cool completely on the pan, then transfer it to a covered container or zippered plastic bag. Store unrefrigerated for up to 2 weeks. Serve with half-and-half, if desired.

Nutritional information per serving:
Carbohydrates: 9 grams; Effective Carb Count: 4 grams; Protein: 8 grams; Fat: 21 grams; Calories: 240

QUESADILLAS IN A RUSH!

Makes 2 servings

A dear friend of mine who is low-carbing makes these little quickies when she is in a rush. She is getting an easy meal without the load of carbs that would normally come from "convenience food."

2 (6") low-carb tortillas
4 ounces cheese, sliced or shredded (Monterey jack, Colby, or a blend)

Place the tortillas on a paper plate. Divide the cheese between the tortillas, putting it on only half of each tortilla. Fold each of the tortillas in half. Microwave them for about 1½ minutes or until they are hot and the cheese is melted. (Don't overcook them or the tortilla will become rubbery.)

Nutritional information per serving:
Carbohydrates: 12 grams; Effective Carb Count: 3 grams;
Protein: 19 grams; Fat: 19 grams; Calories: 272

Reduced-Fat Variation:
Use reduced-fat cheese. Follow all other instructions as given.
Carbohydrates: 13 grams; Effective Carb Count: 4 grams;
Protein: 19 grams; Fat: 6 grams; Calories: 158

QUICK AND EASY LC BREAKFAST SANDWICHES

Makes 2 servings

I don't know anyone who doesn't like breakfast sandwiches! While low-carbers can't eat them at the restaurants because of the biscuits and other fluff they are made of, we can certainly enjoy them at home.

4 slices low-carb bread
1 tablespoon butter
4 slices cheese (any semifirm cheese will work,
though Swiss and Monterey jack are nice!)
1 teaspoon coconut oil
2 eggs
Seasoning salt, to taste
2 sausage patties, cooked, 2 slices ham, or 4 slices bacon, cooked (optional)

1. Toast the bread in a toaster and butter each slice on one side. Place one slice of cheese on each piece of bread.
2. Heat the oil in a skillet over medium heat and fry the eggs, seasoned with seasoning salt, until they are cooked firm. Place one egg on each sandwich.
3. If using the breakfast meat, add it at this point. Either use freshly cooked meat or warm it in the skillet the eggs were cooked in. Divide the meat between the sandwiches. Finish assembling the sandwiches and serve them hot. (You can wrap them deli-style in waxed paper for meals on-the-run!)

Nutritional information per serving:
Carbohydrates: 9 grams; Effective Carb Count: 9 grams;
Protein: 19 grams; Fat: 21 grams; Calories: 302

Reduced-Fat Variation:
Omit the butter and use cooking oil spray instead of the coconut oil.
Optional: Use lean ham. Follow all other directions as given.
Carbohydrates: 9 grams; Effective Carb Count: 9 grams;
Protein: 18 grams; Fat: 13 grams; Calories: 232

Quick and Easy Sausage Gravy

Makes 10 servings

You can make this ahead and reheat only the amount you need. Keep it stored in the fridge for about a week. Serve this yummy gravy hot over eggs, Cauliflower Hash Browns (page 79), or toasted low-carb bread.

1 pound bulk pork sausage
1 (8-ounce) package cream cheese, softened
⅔ cup half-and-half
⅔ cup water
¼ teaspoon seasoning salt
Hot chili oil or freshly ground black pepper (optional)

1. In a medium-sized frying pan over medium heat, cook and crumble the pork sausage until it is no longer pink, about 5 to 8 minutes. Drain off the excess fat.
2. Place the cream cheese in the pan and turn the heat to medium-low. Stir this mixture until the cheese is melted, about a minute. Add the remaining ingredients, stirring constantly to incorporate the liquid into the sausage-cheese mixture. Add additional water if necessary. Add a few drops of hot chili oil, as desired.
3. To reheat, just place the gravy into a microwave-safe container and heat on medium power until it is warm.

Nutritional information per serving:
Carbohydrates: 1 gram; Effective Carb Count: 1 gram;
Protein: 10 grams; Fat: 19 grams; Calories: 220

Reduced-Fat Variation:
Use turkey sausage, low-fat cream cheese, and canned skim milk.
Use very low heat. Follow all remaining instructions as given.
Carbohydrates: 3 grams; Effective Carb Count: 3 grams;
Protein: 10 grams; Fat: 14 grams; Calories: 181

SAUSAGE AND CHEESE MUFFINS

Makes 12 muffins

This is my answer to the "all in one" breakfast sandwich. Make a double batch and pop them into the freezer. Give them a zap in the microwave and you're all set for the day! As with any of my recipes, you may substitute the vital wheat gluten flour equally for soy protein isolate if you have a wheat intolerance.

Dry ingredients:
1 cup ground almonds
¾ cup soy protein isolate
2 tablespoons vital wheat gluten flour
½ teaspoon salt
1 teaspoon baking powder
½ teaspoon baking soda
1 teaspoon parsley flakes
½ teaspoon garlic granules
1 teaspoon dried onion flakes
¾ cup shredded cheese (Cheddar, Colby, or Monterey jack)

Wet ingredients:
1 cup kefir or buttermilk
2 eggs
2 tablespoons olive oil
¾ cup sausage, crumbled and cooked
3 tablespoons (approximately) grated Parmesan cheese
Cooking oil spray

1. Preheat oven to 400°F.
2. Combine the dry ingredients in a large mixing bowl, mixing them well.
3. Combine the wet ingredients *except* the Parmesan cheese and cooking oil spray in a small bowl, mixing them well.
4. Stir the wet ingredients into the dry ingredients, mixing until they are just combined. Do not overmix the batter.
5. Spoon the batter into muffin cups sprayed with cooking oil spray. Top the batter with the Parmesan cheese.
6. Bake the muffins until they are just becoming golden brown, about 18 minutes. Remove them from the pan and let them cool on a rack, or serve them immediately with butter.
7. The muffins may be stored in sealed containers for several days in the refrigerator, or they may be frozen in freezer bags for up to 1 month. To reheat, place the muffins in the microwave on a paper towel, and heat them on medium heat until they are just warmed. (Do not overheat the muffins or they will become rubbery!)

Nutritional information per serving:
Carbohydrates: 3 grams; Effective Carb Count: 2 grams;
Protein: 16 grams; Fat: 18 grams; Calories: 241

Reduced-Fat Variation:
*Use reduced-fat cheese, low-fat buttermilk, and
turkey sausage. Follow all remaining instructions as given.*
Carbohydrates: 4 grams; Effective Carb Count: 3 grams;
Protein: 17 grams; Fat: 13 grams; Calories: 195

SERENDIPITY BAKED PANCAKE

Makes 12 servings

One of my faithful recipe testers made up a batch of Bubby's Buttermilk Flapjacks (page 33) and stuck half of the batter into his freezer. He accidentally microwaved his pancake batter. Capitalizing on his mistake, he continued to cook it until it was nearly done, then drizzled it with sugar-free syrup and enjoyed his new dessert! After he told me about it, his little mistake got me thinking, and this is what I came up with. You can omit the berries and use other flavors of syrup. You could swirl ½ teaspoon cinnamon into some caramel-flavored sugar-free syrup for a delicious variation. The basic recipe is great, so get creative!

Dry ingredients:
1 cup vital wheat gluten flour
1 cup ground almonds
1¼ teaspoons baking soda
¾ teaspoon baking powder
1 teaspoon sea salt
2 packets sucralose or ½ teaspoon SteviaPlus

Wet ingredients:
2 eggs
2 cups kefir or buttermilk
¼ cup butter, melted
½ cup blueberries
Cooking oil spray
¼ cup sugar-free huckleberry-flavored syrup

1. Preheat the oven to 425°F. Combine the dry ingredients in a large mixing bowl. Set them aside.
2. In a smaller bowl, combine the wet ingredients except the syrup and cooking oil spray, mixing them well. Pour the wet ingredients into the dry ingredients and stir them until they are just combined.
3. Pour the batter into a 9" x 13" x 2" pan that has been sprayed with cooking oil spray. Spread the batter evenly in the pan.
4. Drizzle with the syrup, and use a knife to swirl through the batter.
5. Bake it until it is golden brown, about 25 minutes.
6. Serve it with butter and sugar-free specialty syrup. My favorite combination is to spread it with peanut butter then pour caramel-flavored syrup over the top!

Nutritional information per serving:
Carbohydrates: 5 grams; Effective Carb Count: 4 grams; Protein: 21 grams; Fat: 13 grams; Calories: 217

Reduced-Fat Variation:
Use low-fat buttermilk. Use applesauce in place of the butter. Follow all remaining instructions as given.
Carbohydrates: 7 grams; Effective Carb Count: 6 grams; Protein: 21 grams; Fat: 8 grams; Calories: 179

SHARRON'S PORK SAUSAGE

Makes 12 servings

Why am I offering a sausage recipe when it is so readily available at the grocery store? Most commercial sausages have nitrates and other nasty preservatives in them. If you don't have access to fresh sausage without all that yucky stuff, making your own can be a viable alternative. Besides that, it tastes really good! If you like Italian sausage, simply add ½ tablespoon Italian seasonings to the sausage. If you like it spicy, double the lemon pepper and add ½ tablespoon red pepper flakes.

2 pounds ground pork
2 cloves garlic, minced or ½ teaspoon garlic granules
(but fresh is always best!)
½–1 teaspoon fennel or anise seeds
1 teaspoon seasoning salt
1 tablespoon dried minced onion
½ teaspoon lemon pepper
½ teaspoon ground sage
¼ teaspoon SteviaPlus or ½ packet sucralose
½ teaspoon hot chili oil or 1 pinch cayenne
¼ teaspoon dried thyme
¼ teaspoon dried marjoram

1. Place all the ingredients into a deep mixing bowl and combine them thoroughly.
2. You may either crumble the sausage and pan-fry it, or it can be made into patties and baked at 325°F for about 15 minutes or until firm and browned.
3. To freeze the sausage as patties, form the patties and place them onto a baking sheet sprayed with cooking oil spray. Place the baking sheet into the freezer until the sausage is frozen thoroughly. Transfer the sausage into zippered freezer bags and freeze for later use.

>>

4. To cook the frozen sausage patties, place them on a baking sheet and bake them for about 25 minutes or until they are firm and browned.
5. To freeze the sausage in crumbled form, just cook it as in step 2. Freeze as in step 3. Thaw and use as desired.

Nutritional information per serving:
Carbohydrates: 1 gram; Effective Carb Count: 0 grams;
Protein: 13 grams; Fat: 16 grams; Calories: 204

Reduced-Fat Variation:
Use ground chicken, turkey, or lean ground beef.
Follow all other instructions as given. The nutritional
information below has been calculated using turkey.
Carbohydrates: 1 gram; Effective Carb Count: 0 grams;
Protein: 16 grams; Fat: 6 grams; Calories: 113

Even if you are "brown baggin' it," that doesn't mean you have to eat boring food! Meals can always be delicious and nutritious.

Salads and Dressings

2

Q
M

BACON RANCH SALAD DRESSING

Makes 16 servings

Enjoy this easy dressing on Chicken Club Salad (page 61) or use it as a dipping sauce for your favorite meats and veggies. As always, try to use bacon without nitrates, as it seems more and more folks are sensitive to the nitrates.

2 slices cooked bacon or 2 tablespoons real bacon bits
1 packet ranch-flavored salad dressing mix
1 cup mayonnaise
1 cup buttermilk
¼ teaspoon lemon pepper

1. Place the bacon into the chopper of a food processor. Process until it is finely chopped.
2. Place the bacon and all of the remaining ingredients into a bowl and mix them well with a wire whisk. Store the dressing covered in the refrigerator for up to 2 weeks.

Nutritional information per serving:
Carbohydrates: 2 grams; Effective Carb Count: 2 grams;
Protein: 1 gram; Fat: 12 grams; Calories: 114

Reduced-Fat Variation:
Use reduced-fat mayonnaise and buttermilk, and turkey bacon.
Follow all other instructions as given.
Carbohydrates: 4 grams; Effective Carb Count: 4 grams;
Protein: 1 gram; Fat: 3 grams; Calories: 50

CHICKEN CLUB SALAD

Makes 2 servings

This is my version of my favorite fast-food restaurant's best salad. Serve this and you will not feel like you are dieting. You may use bagged salad greens for this recipe. However, I do not recommend iceberg lettuce—it has very little taste and even less nutritional value compared to other types of lettuce.

4 cups torn salad greens
½ cup sliced cucumbers
4 red onion rings
8 cherry or grape tomatoes
4 ounces chicken, cooked, cubed
2 slices cooked bacon (without nitrates, if possible), chopped
2 tablespoons shredded cheese (Colby or Cheddar)
2 tablespoons Ranch Almonds (page 198), sliced
1 recipe Bacon Ranch Salad Dressing (page 60)

1. Rinse the greens and allow them to drain. Place them into two large single-serving salad bowls.
2. Top the salad with the remaining ingredients in the order listed. Enjoy!

Nutritional information per serving (2, not including the dressing):
Carbohydrates: 7 grams; Effective Carb Count: 3 grams; Protein: 15 grams; Fat: 17 grams; Calories: 233

Reduced-Fat Variation:
Use reduced-fat cheese, turkey bacon, and the reduced-fat variation for the Bacon Ranch Salad Dressing. Follow all other instructions as given.
Carbohydrates: 7 grams; Effective Carb Count: 3 grams; Protein: 15 grams; Fat: 15 grams; Calories: 214

CHICKEN WALDORF SALAD

Makes 4 servings

This is a yummy meal for sultry summer nights when it is just too hot to cook! This also makes a great portable meal for lunch on the run. If your carb allowance isn't high enough to use the apple, you may substitute a young zucchini instead.

Salad ingredients:
2 large cooked chicken breasts, cut up
1 medium-sized apple, skin on, cut up
4 stalks celery, cut up (about 1 cup)
½ cucumber, peeled and chopped
½ cup pecan or walnut pieces, broken
½ cup grapes, halved

Dressing ingredients:
¼ cup mayonnaise
¼ cup yogurt
1 teaspoon fresh-squeezed lemon juice
¼ teaspoon SteviaPlus
¼ teaspoon lemon pepper

1. Combine the salad ingredients in a serving bowl.
2. Mix together the dressing ingredients in a small bowl, then pour it over the salad. Mix well. Serve immediately or chill for later use.

Nutritional information per serving:
Carbohydrates: 10 grams; Effective Carb Count: 7 grams;
Protein: 16 grams; Fat: 22 grams; Calories: 294

Reduced-Fat Variation:
Use reduced-fat mayonnaise and low-fat yogurt in the dressing.
Follow all remaining instructions as given.
Carbohydrates: 13 grams; Effective Carb Count: 10 grams;
Protein: 16 grams; Fat: 13 grams; Calories: 229

CLUBHOUSE SAUCE

Makes 16 servings

This is a terrific, versatile sauce that can be used on the Clubhouse Omelette (page 37) or as a sauce for just about any dressing or dipping purpose. It is even great on asparagus. Enjoy! If you want to try alternate sauce bases, like Roquefort or blue cheese, you can get the better quality dressings from your produce department and replace the mayonnaise with the commercial dressing, omitting the ranch packet for another twist on this delicious and versatile sauce.

1 packet ranch-flavored salad dressing mix
1 cup mayonnaise
1 cup buttermilk
¼ teaspoon turmeric
¼ teaspoon chipotle pepper granules or hot chili oil
½ teaspoon paprika
1 teaspoon Old Bay Seasoning

Combine all the ingredients in a mixing bowl or in a salad-dressing shaker; whisk or shake well. Chill the sauce and serve it as a dressing or sauce, as desired.

Nutritional information per serving:
Carbohydrates: 2 grams; Effective Carb Count: 2 grams;
Protein: 1 gram; Fat: 12 grams; Calories: 110

Reduced-Fat Variation:
Use reduced-fat mayonnaise.
Follow all other instructions as given.
Carbohydrates: 4 grams; Effective Carb Count: 4 grams;
Protein: 1 gram; Fat: 3 grams; Calories: 46

CREAMY COCONUT CHICKEN SALAD

Makes 2 to 4 servings, depending upon appetite!

This can be served as a nice summer dinner, or you can make it ahead of time and take it with you on the go!

For the dressing:
½ cup coconut milk
1 tablespoon fresh-squeezed lime juice
½ teaspoon seasoning salt
¼ teaspoon mustard powder
½ teaspoon Sweet & Slender
½ teaspoon grated lime rind (zest)
½ teaspoon parsley flakes

For the salad:
1 head romaine lettuce, cut up
1 large cucumber, sliced
1 bunch radishes, sliced
4 green onions, chopped
1 pound cooked chicken, cut up
4 tablespoons unsweetened shredded coconut
4 tablespoons sunflower seeds, roasted and salted, or hulled pumpkin
seeds, roasted and salted
Lime wedges, for garnish

1. In a small bowl, whisk together the dressing ingredients.
2. Arrange the lettuce on serving plates, covering each with the cucumbers, radishes, onions, and chicken. Pour the dressing over the salads. Garnish each with the coconut, sunflower seeds, and lime wedges. Serve immediately.

Nutritional information per serving
(if you make it for 4):
Carbohydrates: 13 grams; Effective Carb Count: 6 grams;
Protein: 23 grams; Fat: 21 grams; Calories: 321

EGG SALAD

Makes 6 servings

This salad is very yummy stuffed in celery sticks or eaten as a sandwich with low-carb bread. It is a great component for a portable meal!

6 eggs, hard boiled
⅓ cup mayonnaise
½ tablespoon dried onion flakes
Seasoning salt, to taste
Lemon pepper, to taste
1 teaspoon parsley flakes
5 drops hot chili oil or a few grains of cayenne

1. Place the eggs into a pot and add enough cold water to cover them. Add a pinch of salt to the water. (This helps keep the shells from cracking.) Bring the water to a boil over medium heat, then turn off the heat and let them rest undisturbed for about 10 minutes. Drain, and immerse the eggs in cold water.
2. Peel the eggs and mash them using a potato masher or a fork. Stir in the rest of the ingredients. Adjust seasonings to taste.

Nutritional information per serving:
Carbohydrates: 1 gram; Effective Carb Count: 0 grams;
Protein: 6 grams; Fat: 15 grams; Calories: 155

Reduced-Fat Variation:
Use reduced-fat mayonnaise.
Follow all remaining instructions as given.
Carbohydrates: 3 grams; Effective Carb Count: 2 grams;
Protein: 6 grams; Fat: 7 grams; Calories: 98

ITALIAN CHICKEN PASTA SALAD Á LA MAGGIE

Makes 12 side dish or 6 main course servings

I had some ideas for an Italian-type pasta salad, and mentioned it to one of my recipe testers. She told me she already had a really good one worked out. This great salad is superb when taken to a buffet or used for a packed lunch.

For the dressing:
½ cup walnuts, broken up (not chopped)
2 jars red pimientos, cut into strips (about 1" by ¼")
3 tablespoons chopped Italian flat-leaf parsley
or 1½ tablespoons dried parsley
1 cup black olives, pitted and cut into halves
½ cup extra-virgin olive oil
2 tablespoons fresh-squeezed lemon juice
2 teaspoons Frank's RedHot or your favorite hot sauce
¼–½ teaspoon (to taste) garlic powder
Freshly ground black pepper, to taste

For the salad:
6 ounces low-carb pasta
(Darielle brand's fusilli pasta is particularly nice)
3 cups cubed chicken, cooked,
or 3 (4½-ounce) cans oil-packed tuna, drained
4 ounces Swiss cheese, finely grated

1. Combine all the dressing ingredients in a large serving bowl, mixing well.
2. Cook the pasta according to package directions.
3. Drain the pasta and add it to the bowl with the dressing while it is still hot; mix well. Gently stir in the chicken. After the salad has cooled a bit, add the cheese. (You don't want the cheese to melt!)
4. Let stand unrefrigerated for about 20 minutes before serving.

Nutritional information per serving (12 servings):
Carbohydrates: 7 grams; Effective Carb Count: 4 grams;
Protein: 19 grams; Fat: 23 grams; Calories: 294

PIZZA SALAD

Makes 2 servings

Believe it or not, sometimes I get inspired and just sit and dream up recipes. *Oh! This sounds good!* I'll think to myself, and then I'll type it up. This recipe is the result of one such inspiration. As a friend of mine said of this salad, "Pizza and salad! What's not to love?!"

6 cups chopped romaine lettuce

Meat choices (use 4 ounces total of any of the following):
Chicken, cooked and cubed
Beef steak, cooked and cut up
Sausage, cooked and cut up or crumbled
Ham or Canadian bacon, diced
Pepperoni or Salami, diced
Salad shrimp
Bacon, cooked and cut up

Topping choices (use several of the following):
1 tablespoon sliced olives
1 tablespoon chopped bell peppers
6 cherry or grape tomatoes
2 tablespoons mushrooms, sliced (fresh or canned)
2 tablespoons green onion, chopped
1 tablespoon pineapple tidbits, drained
1 tablespoon Parmesan cheese, grated or shredded
2 tablespoons grated mozzarella cheese

Dressing ingredients:
1½ tablespoons red wine vinegar
3 tablespoons olive oil
½ teaspoon Italian seasoning
¼ teaspoon lemon pepper
½ teaspoon seasoning salt

1. Place the lettuce into a large serving bowl. Top it with the desired meat and toppings.
2. In a small dish, combine all the dressing ingredients. Drizzle the dressing over the salad just before serving.

**Nutritional information per serving
(with chicken, mozzarella, olives, mushrooms,
and pineapple for toppings):**
Carbohydrates: 7 grams; Effective Carb Count: 4 grams;
Protein: 17 grams; Fat: 25 grams; Calories: 309

POTLUCK BROCCOLI SALAD

Makes 8 servings

I tasted a salad similar to this for the first time at, you guessed it, a potluck. The version I sampled was sweetened with real sugar, of course. I've tweaked it a bit to suit my tastes. I hope you like it as much as my family does! If you like, you can use some roasted sunflower seeds as a garnish.

Salad ingredients:
6 cups broccoli, finely chopped (or a combo of broccoli and cauliflower)
⅓ cup grated Colby jack or Cheddar cheese
⅓ cup bacon, cooked and chopped
½ cup celery, chopped

Dressing ingredients:
½ cup mayonnaise
1 tablespoon fresh-squeezed lime juice
½ teaspoon Sweet & Slender
½ teaspoon SteviaPlus
¼ teaspoon lemon pepper
2 tablespoons half-and-half

1. Place the salad ingredients into a serving bowl.
2. Combine the dressing ingredients in a small dish. Pour the dressing over the salad and mix it well. Serve at once or refrigerate for up to 3 days.

Nutritional information per serving:
Carbohydrates: 10 grams; Effective Carb Count: 5 grams;
Protein: 4 grams; Fat: 18 grams; Calories: 237

Reduced-Fat Variation:
Use turkey bacon, reduced-fat cheese and reduced-fat mayonnaise instead of those listed. Follow all other remaining instructions as given.
Carbohydrates: 13 grams; Effective Carb Count: 8 grams;
Protein: 3 grams; Fat: 6 grams; Calories: 130

Sesame Spinach Salad

Makes 2 small servings

Why do I so often choose spinach rather than iceberg lettuce for my salads? The reason is twofold: nutrition and taste. Iceberg lettuce just doesn't have much to it nutritionally, whereas spinach is a powerhouse! It contains 70 percent of the recommended daily allowance of vitamin A in just 1½ cups. Eat up! If you use mature spinach, you may need to double the dressing because it has more bulk than baby leaves do.

Dressing ingredients:
1 tablespoon fresh-squeezed lime juice
1½ teaspoons sesame oil
4 drops hot chili oil or a few grains of cayenne
⅛ teaspoon seasoning salt
⅛ teaspoon lemon pepper
⅛ teaspoon Sweet & Slender
1 teaspoon sesame seeds

Salad ingredients:
4 cups baby spinach leaves
2 tablespoons chopped fresh chives
¼ cup fresh bean sprouts or shoots

1. In a small dish, combine the dressing ingredients.
2. In a large bowl, combine the salad ingredients. Drizzle the salad with the dressing and serve immediately.

Nutritional information per serving:
Carbohydrates: 4 grams; Effective Carb Count: 2 grams; Protein: 2 grams; Fat: 5 grams; Calories: 62

SPINACH SALAD WITH STRAWBERRIES

Makes 4 servings

The sun shines high in the sky with its golden beams smiling down on the bright flowers. Dragonflies zip past, while wandering bumblebees light from blossom to blossom. Smells of barbecues tease the nostrils. At the market, the spinach is fresh and crisp. The strawberries are sweet and seem as if they are dripping with honey. These are the days of summer!

Dressing ingredients:
1½ tablespoons fresh-squeezed lemon juice
⅛ teaspoon ground ginger
½ teaspoon grated orange rind (zest)
½ teaspoon Sweet & Slender
1 tablespoon freshly chopped parsley (preferred)
or ½ tablespoon dried parsley
½ teaspoon lemon pepper
3 tablespoons olive oil
4 drops hot chili oil or a few grains of cayenne

Salad ingredients:
6 cups fresh spinach, washed and torn
⅔ cup sliced strawberries (about 6 whole)
2 radishes, sliced
1 green onion, chopped
3 tablespoons hulled pumpkin seeds

1. In a small bowl, combine the dressing ingredients thoroughly.
2. Place the prepared spinach in a serving bowl. Toss it with the salad dressing. Garnish the salad with the remaining ingredients.

Nutritional information per serving:
Carbohydrates: 6 grams; Effective Carb Count: 4 grams;
Protein: 5 grams; Fat: 15 grams; Calories: 170

Q

Sweet-and-Tangy Spinach Salad

Makes 4 servings

I love this salad! It is so easy to prepare and so yummy to eat. You may vary the toppings, as you desire. Only the spinach and the dressing are essential. You may wish to add up to 2 packets of sucralose or double the Sweet & Slender if the dressing is too tangy for your taste.

Dressing ingredients:
3 tablespoons red wine vinegar
2 tablespoons olive oil
½ teaspoon seasoning salt
¼ teaspoon lemon pepper
¼ teaspoon Sweet & Slender

Salad ingredients:
1 (5-ounce) bag baby spinach leaves or 1 bunch spinach,
washed and torn
1 medium-sized avocado, cut up
3 tablespoons Zingy Pumpkin Kernels (page 210)

1. In a small dish combine the dressing ingredients. Set the dressing aside.
2. Place the spinach in a serving bowl. Carefully arrange the avocado slices on top of the spinach and drizzle the dressing over the top. Garnish with the pumpkin kernels.

Nutritional information per serving:
Carbohydrates: 7 grams; Effective Carb Count: 5 grams;
Protein: 3 grams; Fat: 18 grams; Calories: 185

TACO SALAD TILIKUM

Makes 6 servings

I worked in the food service department of a beautiful retreat center when I was first married. One of our favorite lunches to serve was Taco Salad. It was fun to watch the different methods folks used to make their meals. Some would mound the lettuce high, load it with toppings, and finish off with the chips on top. Others, myself included, started with the chips on the bottom and made it more like a nacho salad. You can even prep everything ahead of time to be served later. However you do it, you'll need plenty of napkins for this one!

3 cups Beef and Refried Beans (page 112), heated (about ½ recipe)
1 head romaine lettuce, chopped
1½ cups shredded cheese (Cheddar, Colby, or a Mexican blend)
1 (6-ounce) can olives, drained and sliced
2 large tomatoes, chopped
¾ cup salsa or hot sauce
¾ cup sour cream
Low-Carb Tortilla Chips (page 194), optional

1. Place each of the ingredients in individual serving dishes.
2. Give each guest a plate and instruct them to build their salads. Generally, start with either chips or lettuce on the bottom, then beef/beans, cheese, lettuce, tomatoes, chips, salsa, and sour cream.

Nutritional information per serving:
Carbohydrates: 12 grams; Effective Carb Count: 5 grams;
Protein: 26 grams; Fat: 33 grams; Calories: 431

Reduced-Fat Variation:
*Use the reduced-fat variation of Beef and Refried Beans
(page 112), reduced-fat cheese, and reduced-fat sour cream.
Follow all other instructions as given.*
Carbohydrates: 12 grams; Effective Carb Count: 5 grams;
Protein: 26 grams; Fat: 15 grams; Calories: 274

VERY VEGGIE WRAPS

Makes 2 servings

These are like the vegetarian wraps you will find in many delicatessens. If you like, you may add 2 ounces cooked chicken to the wraps for an extra protein boost. For a delicious variation, try these with Bacon Ranch Salad Dressing (page 60) or Clubhouse Sauce (page 63), Parmesan cheese, baby spinach leaves, sliced black olives, and sunflower seeds. Yummy!

2 (6") low-carb tortillas
3 tablespoons Spinach Dip (page 206)
2 ounces Monterey jack cheese, sliced or shredded
¼ cup sliced cucumber
2 tablespoons sliced radishes
¼ cup alfalfa sprouts
1 small tomato, sliced

1. Lay the tortillas on a work surface. Spread half of each tortilla with the Spinach Dip (page 206), leaving about ½" around the edge uncovered. The dip will spread as you roll the sandwiches.
2. Layer the remaining ingredients on top of the dip. Gently roll the wraps from the filled side to the unfilled side.
3. Eat immediately or wrap them in waxed paper and pack them to go!

Nutritional information per serving:
Carbohydrates: 15 grams; Effective Carb Count: 6 grams; Protein: 13 grams; Fat: 20 grams; Calories: 269

Reduced-Fat Variation:
Use the reduced-fat variation of the Spinach Dip (page 206) and use reduced-fat cheese. Follow all remaining instructions as given.
Carbohydrates: 17 grams; Effective Carb Count: 8 grams; Protein: 12 grams; Fat: 8 grams; Calories: 167

3

Quick and Easy Veggies

BAKED WINTER SQUASH

Number of servings varies according to the size and type of squash

I like to keep cooked winter squash on hand for easy meals. I have it all seasoned in the refrigerator, then I use it either as an easy side dish or as a base for a quick sauce. To separate the "noodles" in spaghetti squash, use a large fork to scrape the flesh from the rind of the squash. For hash browns, prepare as in Cauliflower Hash Browns (page 79). You can also use SteviaPlus, sucralose, and cinnamon instead of the lemon pepper and garlic salt to make a sweetened version.

1 medium-sized squash
(spaghetti, pumpkin, or other winter variety squash)
Butter
Lemon pepper
Garlic salt or seasoning salt

1. Using a sharp utility knife, poke 8 to 10 holes total around the entire circumference of the squash. Place the squash on a baking sheet and bake at 350°F for about 1 hour.
2. Remove from oven and let it rest 5 to 10 minutes before cutting it in half, lengthwise. Scoop out the seeds. (If desired, rinse the seeds and allow them to air dry to use for Zingy Pumpkin Kernels, page 210). Scoop the squash flesh into a serving dish.
3. Add a generous amount of butter, garlic salt, and lemon pepper to the squash and mix well. (The amount of butter and seasonings will vary according to the size and type of squash cooked—you will just have to taste it!)

Nutritional information per serving
(1 cup spaghetti squash and 1 teaspoon butter):
Carbohydrates: 7 grams; Effective Carb Count: 7 grams;
Protein: 1 gram; Fat: 4 grams; Calories: 65

BUTTER-BROWNED ALMONDS

Makes 4 servings

Use this yummy topping to add excitement to your veggies. It is an important part of Wice a Woni (page 101), but it is also wonderful on buttered asparagus, Brussels sprouts, and spinach.

½ tablespoon butter
¼ cup almonds, sliced or slivered
¼ teaspoon seasoning salt

Place all of the ingredients into a small pan and heat them over medium heat, stirring frequently, until they are golden, about 8 minutes. Serve over your favorite veggies.

Nutritional information per serving:
Carbohydrates: 2 grams; Effective Carb Count: 1 gram;
Protein: 2 grams; Fat: 6 grams; Calories: 65

CAULI MASH

Makes 8 servings

Rice, potatoes, bread, etc. My kids call it "real food." I've found that I really don't miss those foods at all! This recipe goes a ways to help fill that potato void, though. My family enjoys the lumpy texture. If you prefer a smoother mash, blend the mixture in a food processor and process it until it is smooth instead of mashing it as instructed in step 2.

2 pounds cauliflower, frozen or fresh
4 ounces (½ cup) cream cheese, softened
1 tablespoon butter
½ teaspoon seasoning salt

Optional toppings:
Sweet onion, chopped
Bacon, cooked and chopped
Cheddar cheese, grated

1. Cook the cauliflower in a covered pot with about 1" water until soft, about 10 minutes.
2. Drain the cauliflower well and mash it with a potato masher. Mash in the cream cheese, butter, and seasoning salt until well combined.
3. Serve hot with the optional toppings on the side.

Nutritional information per serving:
Carbohydrates: 6 grams; Effective Carb Count: 3 grams;
Protein: 3 grams; Fat: 7 grams; Calories: 91

Reduced-Fat Variation:
Use reduced-fat cream cheese and omit the butter.
Use turkey bacon and reduced-fat cheese for the toppings.
Follow the remaining instructions as given.
Carbohydrates: 6 grams; Effective Carb Count: 3 grams;
Protein: 4 grams; Fat: 4 grams; Calories: 65

CAULIFLOWER HASH BROWNS

Makes 2 servings

When I was in college, I frequented the cafeteria in the student union building often. They served amazing biscuits or hash browns and gravy. For the most part, those foods are not a part of the low-carb way of eating . . . until now! This makes a great base for Quick and Easy Sausage Gravy (page 51).

2 tablespoons lard
1 tablespoon butter
⅓ cup chopped onion
Seasoning salt, to taste
3 cups chopped cauliflower (cut into about ½" dice)
¼ teaspoon paprika
Lemon pepper, to taste

1. In a medium-sized frying pan, melt the lard and butter over medium heat. Add the onion, sprinkle with seasoning salt, and cook for about 8 minutes or until the onion turns golden brown.
2. Add the cauliflower to the pan, sprinkle with the paprika, and season liberally with seasoning salt and lemon pepper. Cook over medium heat for about 15 minutes, stirring occasionally.

Nutritional information per serving:
Carbohydrates: 10 grams; Effective Carb Count: 6 grams;
Protein: 3 grams; Fat: 19 grams; Calories: 215

Reduced-Fat Variation:
Use about 2 tablespoons Rich Stock (page 166) to cook the onions. Spray the pan with cooking oil spray to cook the hash browns. Follow the remaining instructions as given.
Carbohydrates: 10 grams; Effective Carb Count: 6 grams;
Protein: 3 grams; Fat: 0; Calories: 48

Easy Cream Sauce

Makes about 8 servings

This versatile sauce can be used "as is," as Alfredo sauce or as cheese sauce. It is great served over broccoli, cauliflower, asparagus, Brussels sprouts, etc. If you choose xanthan gum as your thickener, it will reheat better, but I prefer the taste of the arrowroot as a thickener.

1½ teaspoons butter
1½ teaspoons coconut oil
4 cloves garlic, minced
½ teaspoon seasoning salt
1 cup half-and-half
½ teaspoon xanthan gum or about 1 teaspoon arrowroot
½ cup shredded cheese (Colby, Cheddar, or Parmesan)—optional
Nutmeg, if using Parmesan cheese

1. Melt the butter and coconut oil in a small saucepan over medium heat. Add the garlic and sauté until fragrant.
2. Add the seasoning salt and ¾ cup of the half-and-half; cook until bubbling.
3. Mix the thickener with the remaining ¼ cup half-and-half. Add it to the bubbling sauce in the pot, stirring lightly. Turn off the heat and add the cheese, if using it.
4. Pour the sauce over your veggies and garnish with nutmeg if using Parmesan cheese. The total cooking time is about 10 minutes.

Nutritional information per serving (with Parmesan):
Carbohydrates: 2 grams; Effective Carb Count: 2 grams; Protein: 3 grams; Fat: 7 grams; Calories: 80

Reduced-Fat Variation:
Use canned skim milk instead of the half-and-half.
If using Cheddar cheese, use reduced-fat cheese.
Follow all remaining instructions as given.
Carbohydrates: 5 grams; Effective Carb Count: 5 grams; Protein: 5 grams; Fat: 3 grams; Calories: 65

EASY-PEASY GREENY BEANIES

Makes 4 servings

We had some friends over for dinner and their twelve-year-old daughter said, "Wow! How do you make these beans? They are so good!" I just stared blankly at her. I had simply thrown them together and seasoned them! Here they are, just as easy and yummy for you to enjoy.

> 1 (16-ounce) package frozen cut green beans
> 2 tablespoons butter
> ½ teaspoon seasoning salt
> ¼ teaspoon lemon pepper
> ¼ teaspoon garlic granules

1. Place the green beans into a medium-sized saucepan with a lid. Add about ½" to 1" of water to the pot. Cook the beans, covered, over medium heat for about 10 minutes or until tender. (They should not have that "squeaky" feeling to them!)
2. Drain the beans. Place them in a serving dish and add the butter and seasonings. Stir and serve.

Nutritional information per serving:
Carbohydrates: 9 grams; Effective Carb Count: 6 grams;
Protein: 2 grams; Fat: 6 grams; Calories: 90

GOLDEN ONIONS AND MUSHROOMS

Makes 4 servings

So simple, but so delicious! Serve them atop your favorite steak or chops or as the filling for an omelette.

½ tablespoon butter
1 tablespoon lard
1 medium-sized onion
¾ teaspoon seasoning salt
2 cups mushrooms, sliced

1. In a medium-sized frying pan, melt the butter and the lard. Add the onions and the seasoning salt, and cook over medium heat for about 5 minutes or until the onions are translucent.
2. Add the mushrooms to the pan and cook for about 5 minutes, until golden.

Nutritional information per serving:
Carbohydrates: 5 grams; Effective Carb Count: 4 grams;
Protein: 1 gram; Fat: 5 grams; Calories: 66

Reduced-Fat Variation:
Use 1 teaspoon butter and about 2 tablespoons
Rich Stock (page 166) instead of the butter and lard.
Follow the remaining instructions as given.
Carbohydrates: 5 grams; Effective Carb Count: 4 grams;
Protein: 1 gram; Fat: 1 gram; Calories: 33

GREEN BEAN CASSEROLE

Makes 16 servings

Everyone is familiar with the bean casserole that is typically served around the holidays. Here is a low-carb version that won't break the carb bank! For easy cleanup with this recipe and many other baked dishes, simply line the baking pan with foil before filling it. When it is time to clean up, just lift the foil out for an easy wash job!

Mock Cream of Mushroom Soup (page 89), doubled
2 pounds frozen cut green beans, thawed
1 tablespoon butter
1 cup pecans, broken up
¼ teaspoon seasoning salt
⅛ teaspoon lemon pepper

1. Prepare a double batch of the mushroom soup as directed. Preheat oven to 350°F.
2. Stir the thawed green beans into the soup. Pour that mixture into a 9" x 13" baking pan and smooth the top with the back of a spoon.
3. Place the butter into a microwave-safe bowl that is large enough to hold the remaining ingredients. Heat the butter in the microwave until it melts, about 25 seconds. Stir in the remaining ingredients. Sprinkle the seasoned pecans evenly over the top of the casserole.
4. Bake it at 350°F for about 45 minutes, or until the sauce begins to bubble and the top begins to brown.

Nutritional information per serving:
Carbohydrates: 9 grams; Effective Carb Count: 7 grams;
Protein: 3 grams; Fat: 14 grams; Calories: 163

Reduced-Fat Variation:
Use the reduced-fat variation of the Mock Cream of Mushroom Soup (page 89). Omit the butter in the topping and spray the top with olive oil cooking spray. Follow all remaining instructions as given.
Carbohydrates: 9 grams; Effective Carb Count: 7 grams;
Protein: 3 grams; Fat: 8 grams; Calories: 103

GREEN BEANS WITH PUMPKIN KERNELS AND MUSHROOMS

Makes 6 servings

I was served a sample of some green beans with pine nuts while at a local market. I enjoyed it so much that I wanted to make something similar at home. I didn't have the pine nuts, and I had a half package of sliced mushrooms on hand. I substituted pumpkin kernels for the pine nuts and added in the mushrooms. I like my variation quite well. I hope you do, too!

4 cloves garlic, minced (about 1 tablespoon)
2 tablespoons butter
1 tablespoon olive oil
1 cup sliced mushrooms
1 teaspoon seasoning salt
½ teaspoon lemon pepper
⅓ cup raw pumpkin kernels
1 (16-ounce) package frozen cut green beans

1. Cook the garlic in the butter and olive oil over medium heat until the garlic becomes fragrant, about 4 minutes. Add the mushrooms, seasoning salt, and lemon pepper and cook until the mushrooms are soft.
2. Add the pumpkin kernels and cook for 2 minutes, stirring frequently. Add the green beans and continue to cook, stirring frequently, for about 5 more minutes or until the beans are softened.

Nutritional information per serving:
Carbohydrates: 9 grams; Effective Carb Count: 6 grams;
Protein: 4 grams; Fat: 10 grams; Calories: 129

HERBED CAULIFLOWER

Makes 8 servings

I have pots sitting around my deck filled with herbs. They are so easy to grow! Even if you live in an apartment, you can grow fresh herbs. If you don't have fresh herbs, most markets carry them in their produce section. This dish is great served alongside simple grilled meats or fish.

1 large head cauliflower (about 2½–3 pounds)
1 tablespoon lard or coconut oil
1½ tablespoons olive oil
1 sprig mint (about ½ tablespoon chopped)
1 sprig rosemary (about ½ tablespoon chopped)
1 sprig thyme or lemon thyme (about 1 teaspoon chopped)
1 sprig oregano (about 1 teaspoon chopped)
3 cloves garlic, minced
½ tablespoon grated lemon rind (zest)
½ tablespoon fresh chives, chopped
2 cups fresh spinach, chopped
½ tablespoon fresh-squeezed lemon juice
¾ teaspoon seasoning salt
¼ teaspoon lemon pepper

1. Cut the cauliflower from the stem and place it in a medium-sized saucepan with a lid. Add about ½" of water to the pan. Cook, covered, over medium heat until soft, about 10 to 12 minutes. Drain well.
2. While the cauliflower is cooking, prepare the herb sauce: In a small frying pan, melt the lard and olive oil over medium heat. Add the mint, rosemary, thyme, oregano, garlic, and lemon zest. Cook them for about 5 to 8 minutes, or until the garlic is golden. Add the chives, spinach, lemon juice, and seasonings. Stir while cooking until the spinach wilts, about 2 minutes. Set the herb sauce aside.
3. Transfer the cooked cauliflower to a serving bowl and mash it with a potato masher. Pour the herb sauce over the cauliflower and mix well.

Nutritional information per serving:
Carbohydrates: 9 grams; Effective Carb Count: 5 grams;
Protein: 3 grams; Fat: 5 grams; Calories: 79

LEMON BUTTER

Makes 8 servings

This simple sauce is great served with artichokes, asparagus, Brussels sprouts, shellfish, etc.

¼ cup butter
1½ tablespoons fresh-squeezed lemon juice
Zest of 1 lemon (optional)

Place the butter and lemon juice in a microwave-safe dish. Microwave them on high for about 30 seconds or until the butter is melted. Stir and enjoy!

Nutritional information per serving:
Carbohydrates: 0 grams; Effective Carb Count: 0 grams;
Protein: 0 grams; Fat: 6 grams; Calories: 52

Lori's Parmesan Breading

Makes about 8 servings

This is an easy high-protein topping for veggies, but the breading can even be used on chicken, fish, and pork. Serve with Pizza Sauce (page 158) for dipping.

Breading ingredients:
2 cups grated Parmesan cheese
4 teaspoons Italian seasoning
1 teaspoon garlic powder

Other ingredients:
2 eggs plus 1 tablespoon water
8 ounces veggies suitable for breading
(zucchini, okra, mushrooms, etc.), cut up
Lard, for frying

1. Combine the breading ingredients in a shallow dish. Combine the egg and water in another shallow dish. Dip the veggies first into the egg, then into the breading, coating them well. (Be careful not to overdo it on the egg wash; otherwise you'll end up with a dish of cheesy-goo for your breading!)
2. Meanwhile, melt enough lard to cover the bottom of a medium-sized frying pan about ½" deep.
3. Fry the veggies until they are golden brown and crisp. Serve hot.

Nutritional information per serving (with zucchini):
Carbohydrates: 3 grams; Effective Carb Count: 2 grams;
Protein: 12 grams; Fat: 15 grams; Calories: 192

MEXICAN RICE-AFLOWER

Makes about 10 servings

I'm sure you've been to a nice Mexican restaurant and had their wonderful rice with those just-perfect seasonings. Now, you can enjoy it without the accompanying carb load!

1 head cauliflower (yield about 6 cups chopped, instructions below)
2 tablespoons lard
1 medium-sized onion, chopped
3 cloves garlic, minced, about 1½ tablespoons
½ teaspoon seasoning salt
2 teaspoons chicken bouillon granules
3 tablespoons tomato sauce
1 teaspoon lemon pepper
⅛ teaspoon ground cumin

1. Cut the cauliflower into pieces that will fit into the bowl of a food processor; pulse until it is the consistency of rice. (Do not use a steady chop setting or it won't have the proper texture. You can do it by hand, but be prepared to get very tired!) Set the chopped cauliflower aside.
2. Melt the lard over medium heat in a large frying pan. Add the onion, garlic, and seasoning salt, and cook until they are beginning to brown, about 8 minutes.
3. Add the remaining ingredients and the chopped cauliflower to the pan, stirring well so that all the ingredients are evenly dispersed throughout the "rice." Cook, continuing to stir frequently, for about 5 minutes or until the cauliflower is heated through. Serve hot.
4. This will keep refrigerated for a few days; reheat in the microwave or with a bit of oil in a frying pan over medium heat until it is hot.

Nutritional information per serving:
Carbohydrates: 5 grams; Effective Carb Count: 3 grams;
Protein: 2 grams; Fat: 3 grams; Calories: 47

Mock Cream of Mushroom Soup

Makes 8 servings

I used to use cream of mushroom soup as a base for casseroles and sauces all the time. Once I started on the low-carb lifestyle, though, I gave that up. Now, I can have my favorite sauce standby without the junk that is in canned soups! You can substitute the mushrooms with just about any veggie you would want to make into a cream soup base: Onions, spinach, asparagus, celery, broccoli, etc. This recipe will substitute for one can of soup in many recipes. You can add 1 or 2 eggs if you need it to have more "body" for baking or additional half-and-half if you need it thinner for sauces. Be careful, though, it can't cook for long periods of time or the sauce will break down. It needs to be added to a dish toward the end of the cooking time if it is a stovetop recipe. It bakes just fine.

½ tablespoon lard
1 tablespoon butter
1 cup sliced or chopped mushrooms
½ cup finely chopped onion
½ teaspoon seasoning salt
⅛ teaspoon lemon pepper
1 cup (8 ounces) sour cream
2 tablespoons half-and-half

1. Melt the lard and butter over medium heat in a large frying pan. Add the mushrooms, onion, and seasonings; sauté for about 10 minutes, until the mixture is quite thick. (It will become saucy, then begin to cook down.) Cook off most of the juices from the veggies, but be careful not to cook it until the mixture is completely dry.
2. Pour the veggies into a fairly large bowl and allow them to cool for about 3 minutes. Stir in the sour cream and half-and-half, mixing well. Use as desired.

Nutritional information per serving:
Carbohydrates: 3 grams; Effective Carb Count: 3 grams;
Protein: 1 gram; Fat: 9 grams; Calories: 93

Reduced-Fat Variation:
Use fat-free sour cream and canned skim milk.
Follow all remaining instructions as given.
Carbohydrates: 3 grams; Effective Carb Count: 3 grams;
Protein: 1 gram; Fat: 3 grams; Calories: 39

ONION SOUP

Makes about 6 servings

This can be used as an appetizer or as a light lunch with hard-boiled eggs or cooked chicken on the side. You can also use this as a soup base for making more involved dishes, like stews, soups, and gravies.

1 tablespoon lard or coconut oil
1 tablespoon butter
1 large sweet onion, sliced into strips
4 cloves garlic, minced
2 tablespoons chopped fresh cilantro or Italian flat-leaf parsley
¾ teaspoon seasoning salt
½ teaspoon lemon pepper
6 cups beef-based Rich Stock (page 166) or
commercially prepared beef broth
Sea salt, to taste
Black pepper, to taste
Fresh-grated Parmesan cheese, for garnish (optional)

1. Melt the lard and butter over medium heat in a 5-quart stockpot. Add the onion, garlic, and cilantro, and cook them until the onion is quite golden, about 8 minutes.
2. Add the seasoning salt, lemon pepper, and stock to the pot and simmer the soup for about 20 minutes. Season to taste with sea salt and black pepper. Garnish with Parmesan cheese, if desired.

Nutritional information per serving:
Carbohydrates: 3 grams; Effective Carb Count: 3 grams;
Protein: 1 gram; Fat: 4 grams; Calories: 49

RICE-AFLOWER

Makes 4 servings

I always have at least 1 head of cauliflower in the fridge and at least 1 bag of frozen cauliflower in the freezer. This is one of my busy family's staple veggies! You can also serve this as a base for your gravies and sauces.

½ medium-sized head cauliflower (or the equivalent, frozen)
3 tablespoons butter
¼ teaspoon seasoning salt
Dash lemon pepper (less than ⅛ teaspoon)

1. Cut the cauliflower in 2" chunks and place them into a small saucepan with a tightly fitting lid. Pour about ½" of water into the pan. Cover and bring to a boil over medium heat. Reduce the heat and continue to boil slowly for 8 to 10 minutes or until the cauliflower pierces easily with a fork. (This cooking time is longer than the normal "crisp-tender" stage for cauliflower, but *do not* cook it until it is mushy!)
2. Drain the cauliflower in a colander and transfer it to a bowl. Add the butter, seasoning salt, and lemon pepper. Mash it with a potato masher until the cauliflower is the consistency and texture of rice.

Nutritional information per serving:
Carbohydrates: 5 grams; Effective Carb Count: 2 grams;
Protein: 2 grams; Fat: 9 grams; Calories: 102

Reduced-Fat Variation:
Use 1½ teaspoons butter and follow
the remaining instructions as given.
Carbohydrates: 5 grams; Effective Carb Count: 2 grams;
Protein: 2 grams; Fat: 2 grams; Calories: 38

SHILO VEGGIES

Makes 6 servings

My family went on a trip to the Oregon beach. It was wonderful! We flew kites so high that you could barely see them. We walked on the cool beach and found fossilized seashells and stones. We went to a buffet at a local hotel one night and they served veggies similar to these. These leftovers are great in omelettes.

1 tablespoon olive oil
1 tablespoon coconut oil
1 medium-sized sweet onion, cut into strips
2 cloves garlic, minced
1 teaspoon seasoning salt, divided
1 round summer squash or yellow summer squash,
sliced (about 1½ cups)
2 medium-sized zucchinis, sliced (about 3½ cups)
12 spears asparagus, cut into 1" sections,
or about 1½ cups frozen asparagus pieces
1 teaspoon fresh rosemary, chopped
½ teaspoon lemon pepper
8 drops hot chili oil (about ⅛ teaspoon) or
about 1/16 teaspoon chipotle pepper granules

1. In a large frying pan with a lid, heat the olive oil and coconut oil over medium heat. Add the onion, garlic, and ½ teaspoon of the seasoning salt. Stir them together, then cover and let them steam for about 3 minutes. Uncover the pan and cook until the onion is golden, about 5 minutes total.
2. Add the remaining ingredients, stir well, and cover the pan. Cook, stirring occasionally, for another 5 minutes or so, until the veggies are just tender.
3. Keep leftovers covered and refrigerated for up to 5 days. To reheat, warm them in the microwave until they are hot.

Nutritional information per serving:
Carbohydrates: 7 grams; Effective Carb Count: 4 grams;
Protein: 2 grams; Fat: 5 grams; Calories: 74

Reduced-Fat Variation:
Use 1 teaspoon olive oil, omit the coconut oil, and add olive oil cooking spray, as needed. Follow all remaining instructions as given.
Carbohydrates: 7 grams; Effective Carb Count: 4 grams;
Protein: 2 grams; Fat: 1 gram; Calories: 41

SLURP 'EM UP CABBAGE NOODLES

Makes 6 servings

Kid factor: They slurp just like noodles! You can serve this surprisingly simple and tasty veggie dish as a base for your favorite sauce or gravy.

½ head cabbage
¼ teaspoon lemon pepper
½ teaspoon seasoning salt
¼ cup butter

1. Slice the cabbage into strips about ¼" wide, so they resemble fettuccini noodles. Individually separate the pieces of cabbage so that they are not in clumps or chunks. This will allow the water and steam to cook them evenly.
2. Place the sliced cabbage pieces into a saucepan (or steamer) and add about ½" of water. Cover the pan with a tight-fitting lid, and cook the cabbage on medium heat for about 8 minutes or until tender. (They need to be slightly on the soft side—not the normal "crisp-tender" you would want from a fresh vegetable— in order to achieve the "noodle" feel.)
3. Drain the cabbage thoroughly. Place the butter in the bottom of a serving bowl and sprinkle the lemon pepper and seasoning salt over it. Add the cabbage and mix thoroughly with the butter and seasonings.

Nutritional information per serving:
Carbohydrates: 4 grams; Effective Carb Count: 2 grams;
Protein: 1 gram; Fat: 8 grams; Calories: 87

Reduced-Fat Variation:
Use 2 tablespoons butter. Follow all other instructions as given.
Carbohydrates: 4 grams; Effective Carb Count: 2 grams;
Protein: 1 gram; Fat: 4 grams; Calories: 53

STIR-FRIED VEGGIES

Makes 8 servings

This simple and satisfying side dish is great when served along with plain meat or fish. Sometimes we need to let the veggies be the star of the meal!

Sauce ingredients:
2 tablespoons Bragg Liquid Aminos
½ teaspoon fresh-grated orange rind (zest)
½ teaspoon ground ginger
½ teaspoon Sweet & Slender
¼ teaspoon seasoning salt
¼ teaspoon lemon pepper
¼ teaspoon hot chili oil or about ⅛ teaspoon cayenne
½ teaspoon arrowroot powder

Other ingredients:
2 cloves garlic, minced
2 tablespoons lard or coconut oil
1 small carrot, diced (optional)
2 stalks celery, chopped (about ¾ cup)
3 green onions, chopped, whites and greens separated
4 cups chopped napa cabbage or regular cabbage
2 cups green pea shoots or 1 cup snow peas, cut into ¾" lengths
½ cup bean sprouts

>>

1. Combine the sauce ingredients in a small cup and set them aside.
2. In a large wok or frying pan over high heat, cook the garlic in the lard until it is just becoming fragrant, about 30 seconds. Add the carrot, celery, and whites from the green onions, and cook them for about 2 minutes, stirring constantly with a lifting and scooping motion.
3. Add the remaining veggies, except the green onion tops, and cook for another 1 to 2 minutes, stirring constantly as described in step 2.
4. Stir the sauce into the veggies and let it cook for just a few seconds, until it is thickened. Transfer the veggies to a serving dish and garnish them with the green onion tops.

Nutritional information per serving:
Carbohydrates: 5 grams; Effective Carb Count: 3 grams;
Protein: 1 gram; Fat: 4 grams; Calories: 54

SUMMER SQUASH WITH ONIONS

Makes 6 servings

In the summer, when the squashes first start to come into season, they are dainty and delicate. Their flavor and texture are superb, not bland and spongy like in the late summer when the squashes are huge. My brother always maintained that he didn't care for yellow summer squash, which I found surprising. They are my favorite. Once he tasted this dish, they were his favorite as well! If you opt for using the herbs, it really doesn't matter what kind you choose. All the varieties I've tried have worked well!

1 tablespoon butter
1 tablespoon coconut oil
1 medium-sized onion, cut into strips
3 cloves garlic, minced
2 zucchini (about 6" long), sliced about ¼" to ½" thick
4 small yellow summer squashes (about 4" long),
sliced about ¼" to ½" thick
1 tablespoon chopped fresh herbs (optional)
¾ teaspoon seasoning salt
½ teaspoon lemon pepper
10 drops hot chili oil (about ¼ teaspoon) or about ¹⁄₁₆ teaspoon cayenne

1. In a medium-sized frying pan with a lid, melt the butter with the coconut oil over medium heat; sauté the onion and garlic until almost golden, about 5 minutes.
2. Add the remaining ingredients and stir well. Cover and continue to cook the veggies over medium heat until they are just soft, about 5 to 8 minutes. (You don't want them to become mushy, but they shouldn't be crisp, either.)

Nutritional information per serving:
Carbohydrates: 7 grams; Effective Carb Count: 4 grams;
Protein: 2 grams; Fat: 5 grams; Calories: 72

Reduced-Fat Variation:
Use 1 teaspoon each of butter and coconut oil. Use olive oil cooking spray as necessary to keep the onions and garlic from sticking. Follow all other instructions as given.
Carbohydrates: 7 grams; Effective Carb Count: 4 grams;
Protein: 2 grams; Fat: 2 grams; Calories: 48

VEGGIES, NOW AND LATER

Makes about 8 servings

Package this up once a week and you've got something always ready for when you need some veggies in a rush. I do a lot of my cooking in the once-a-week mode. I'll prepare these veggies, some Bacon Ranch Salad Dressing (page 60), some Easy Lemon Pepper Chicken (page 132), and some grilled steak or Ranch Chops (page 164). It gives this family of 6 enough food for several days, leaving me more time to spend with that family of 6!

1 bunch broccoli
1 small head cauliflower
1 bunch celery
Other veggies you may enjoy, like
zucchini, mushrooms, jicama, etc. (optional)

1. Wash the veggies and allow them to air-dry on towels.
2. Cut the veggies up into serving-size pieces and place them in a large zippered plastic bag. Chill in the refrigerator until ready to use.

Nutritional information per serving:
Carbohydrates: 5 grams; Effective Carb Count: 2 grams;
Protein: 3 grams; Fat: 0 grams; Calories: 25

WICE A WONI

Makes 10 servings

When I was telling my friend that I'd come up with a dish that tasted similar to those popular boxed rice dishes, her eyes bugged out and she said, "Wice a Woni?" I thought that was so cute, I decided to name this recipe after her exclamation!

Quick and Easy Veggies

1 head cauliflower (yield about 6 cups chopped, instructions below)
2 tablespoons lard
1 tablespoon coconut oil
1 medium-sized onion
3 cloves garlic, minced
1 teaspoon seasoning salt, divided
2 teaspoons chicken bouillon granules
1 teaspoon lemon pepper
½ teaspoon celery seeds
¼ teaspoon dried thyme
2 tablespoons dried parsley flakes
⅛ teaspoon paprika
1 recipe Butter-Browned Almonds (page 77)

1. Cut the cauliflower into pieces that will fit into the bowl of a food processor. Pulse it until it is the consistency of rice. (Do not use a steady chop setting or it won't have the proper texture. You can do it by hand, but be prepared to get very tired!) Set aside the chopped cauliflower.
2. Melt the lard and coconut oil over medium heat in a large frying pan. Add the onion, garlic, and ½ teaspoon of the seasoning salt, and cook until lightly browned, about 8 minutes.
3. Add the remaining ingredients to the pan, stirring well to fully incorporate the seasonings into the onion mixture. Add the chopped cauliflower, and stir well. Cook, uncovered, continuing to stir frequently for about 5 minutes or until the cauliflower is heated through.
4. Serve with Butter-Browned Almonds (page 77) as a garnish.

Nutritional information per serving:
Carbohydrates: 5 grams; Effective Carb Count: 3 grams;
Protein: 2 grams; Fat: 6 grams; Calories: 79

Main Courses

4

ADOBO (PORK WITH GRAVY)

Makes 10 servings

Several years ago a dear lady who had lived in the Philippines for several years taught me how to make several Philippine dishes. Adobo was always my favorite of the ones that she taught me. When I wander through the Asian market, I see packets of seasoning mixes for adobo. I think, "Why? It is so easy!" Beef stew meat may also be used for this recipe. Serve this over Rice-Aflower (page 92).

½ tablespoon coconut oil or lard
1 head garlic, minced (yes, head, not clove), about ¼ cup
2½ pounds pork stew meat
¼ cup fresh-squeezed lemon or lime juice or apple cider vinegar
2 bay leaves
1 tablespoon Bragg Liquid Aminos
½ teaspoon sea salt
¼ teaspoon SteviaPlus
½ packet sucralose
1½ cups Rich Stock, pork or beef (page 166),
or commercially prepared broth, or water
½ tablespoon arrowroot, plus 2 tablespoons water
(or about ½ teaspoon xanthan gum)

1. In a deep frying pan with a lid, heat the coconut oil on medium. Add the garlic and sauté until fragrant, about 30 seconds. Add the meat to the pan and brown it, cooking it until it is no longer red. You may cover the pan to speed the cooking time.
2. Add the lemon juice, bay leaves, Bragg, sea salt, sweeteners, and stock. Cover the pan and simmer the gravy until the meat is tender and the broth is rich looking, about 20 minutes to 2 hours. This recipe is very flexible. If you use a more tender cut of meat, it can be ready in 20 minutes. If you use beef stew meat or a tougher cut of pork, you may wish to allow more cooking time. The average is about 40 minutes. Alternatively, you may cook this in a slow cooker on low heat for about 8 hours.

>>

3. When ready to serve the gravy, remove the bay leaves. Stir the arrowroot/water mixture into the bubbling broth, and stir it minimally until it is thickened. Serve immediately.

Nutritional information per serving:
Carbohydrates: 2 grams; Effective Carb Count: 2 grams;
Protein: 17 grams; Fat: 11 grams; Calories: 181

Reduced-Fat Variation:
*Instead of the coconut oil, use olive oil cooking spray
and use equal parts of pork and chicken for the meat.
Follow all remaining instructions as given.*
Carbohydrates: 2 grams; Effective Carb Count: 2 grams;
Protein: 19 grams; Fat: 6 grams; Calories: 141

BARBECUE CHICKEN WITH HERB SMOKE

Serves 4

The herbs on the coals make the chicken have an amazing flavor that is impossible to duplicate any other way. I'll actually cook as much chicken as my barbecue will hold, then we'll eat it all week!

> *1 whole frying chicken, cut into serving pieces,*
> *(or the equivalent in pieces)*
> *Seasoning salt, to taste*
> *Lemon pepper, to taste*
> *2 6"-sprigs fresh herbs (rosemary, thyme, oregano,*
> *French sorrel, or whatever is available)*

1. Prepare medium-hot coals in a barbecue with a cover. Season both sides of the meat liberally with seasoning salt and lemon pepper.
2. Remove the barbecue rack and place the herbs directly on the coals. Place the meat on the highest rack setting (about 5 to 6 inches away from the coals).
3. Cover the barbecue and allow the meat to smoke, turning it occasionally. Cook it for about 45 minutes or until the meat is golden brown and firm to the touch. (Using the meat thermometer is discouraged when barbecuing because those precious juices are lost!)

Nutritional information per serving:
Carbohydrates: 0 grams; Effective Carb Count: 0 grams;
Protein: 32 grams; Fat: 29 grams; Calories: 397

Reduced-Fat Variation:
Remove the skin from the chicken.
Follow all other instructions as given.
Carbohydrates: 0 grams; Effective Carb Count: 0 grams;
Protein: 27 grams; Fat: 5 grams; Calories: 164

BARBECUE MARINADE MADE EASY

Makes about 16 servings
(enough to coat 3 to 4 pounds of meat)

Do you ever thaw out meat then realize you don't know what you are going to do with it? This always seems to happen when we are at our busiest and least creative. This simple marinade is the perfect answer; it is supereasy to throw together and it tastes like a much more complicated teriyaki-type sauce. It goes great with beef ribs, pork chops or ribs, chicken, or turkey.

1½ cups diet lemon cola
1 tablespoon ground ginger
1 teaspoon lemon pepper
½ teaspoon chili pepper flakes
¼ cup Bragg Liquid Aminos

Combine the marinade ingredients in a very large container with a lid. The marinade may be refrigerated up to 2 weeks, unused.

Nutritional information per serving:
This marinade alone has negligible calories and carbs.

BARBECUE SAUCE WITH AN ASIAN FLAIR

Makes about 8 servings

The very first time I made this sauce, I used it on some beef short ribs. I marinated them all day, then baked them, covered, for about 2 hours at 350°F. While they were baking, I received a phone call from a friend inviting my family to a bonfire in the rain. We went and brought our food with us. The ribs and this sauce were a big hit! During the summer months, you may wish to double this recipe so that you have some on hand for those sultry summer barbecues.

½ cup Bragg Liquid Aminos or soy sauce
¼ cup fresh-squeezed lime juice
2 teaspoons garlic granules
2 tablespoons ground ginger
¼ teaspoon SteviaPlus
1 packet sucralose
½ teaspoon ground cloves
½ teaspoon ground cinnamon
¼ teaspoon anise or fennel seeds

Combine all of the ingredients in a small dish or jar, stirring well to break up any lumps. Use as a basting sauce over your favorite meat. This sauce may be kept refrigerated for up to 4 weeks.

Nutritional information per serving:
Carbohydrates: 2 grams; Effective Carb Count: 2 grams;
Protein: 0 grams; Fat: 0 grams; Calories: 10

BASIC RIBS

Makes 6 servings

This functional recipe is a good starting point for many different options. Top it with a 14-ounce can of sauerkraut, Sweet-and-Sour Sauce, Take Two (page 172), Barbecue Sauce with an Asian Flair (page 108), or make a gravy using xanthan gum or arrowroot to thicken the pan drippings. Easy and versatile. My kind of food!

2½ pounds country-style pork ribs (boneless preferred)
Seasoning salt, to taste
Lemon pepper, to taste

1. Cut the ribs into 2" to 3" chunks. Sprinkle them liberally with the seasonings.
2. Place the meat into a broiler-safe baking pan. Broil on all sides until the fat is bubbling, about 8 minutes total.
3. Reduce the heat to 350°F and bake the ribs for about 30 minutes.
4. Coat the ribs with the sauce of your choice, then cover the pan with foil. At this point, the ribs may be refrigerated until ready to use. When you are ready, bake them, covered, at 350°F for about 45 minutes if refrigerated, 30 minutes if not. If you have time, you can bake them for up to 1½ hours to make the meat really tender.

Nutritional information per serving:
Carbohydrates: 0 grams; Effective Carb Count: 0 grams;
Protein: 22 grams; Fat: 24 grams; Calories: 310

BEEF AND BROCCOLI IN A SNAP!

Makes 8 servings

One of my favorite meals at a Chinese restaurant is beef and broccoli. When I'm there, I ask for "no gravy" and "no sugar," so they don't use the thickener or put sugar in my food. When I make it at home, I don't have those concerns!

1 tablespoon coconut oil or lard
1½ pounds top sirloin, or other appropriate cut,
beef steak, cut into strips
¾ teaspoon seasoning salt
1 teaspoon garlic granules
¼ teaspoon ground ginger
¼ teaspoon lemon pepper
1 (2-pound) bag frozen chopped broccoli
3 tablespoons Bragg Liquid Aminos or soy sauce
8 drops hot chili oil (about ⅛ teaspoon)
or about ¹⁄₁₆ teaspoon cayenne or chipotle pepper granules
1½ teaspoons sesame oil
Sesame seeds, for garnish

1. Place a wok or other very large skillet over high heat on the stove. Add the coconut oil. As soon as it is melted, add the beef and seasonings, stirring well to coat the meat evenly. Do not cover the pan at this point. Continue cooking the meat, using a lifting and stirring motion, until it is no longer red.
2. Add the frozen broccoli to the pan and stir it well. Cover and allow it to steam for about 3 to 5 minutes, stirring occasionally, until the broccoli is heated through.
3. Add the Bragg, chili oil, and sesame oil to the pan. Stir well, continuing to use the same lifting and stirring motion described in step 1.
4. Transfer the hot food to a serving dish and top with sesame seeds, if desired.

>>

Nutritional information per serving:
Carbohydrates: 6 grams; Effective Carb Count: 3 grams;
Protein: 20 grams; Fat: 7 grams; Calories: 159

Reduced-Fat Variation:
Use olive oil cooking spray instead of the coconut oil.
Follow all other instructions as given.
Carbohydrates: 6 grams; Effective Carb Count: 3 grams;
Protein: 20 grams; Fat: 5 grams; Calories: 145

BEEF AND REFRIED BEANS

Makes 10 servings

This is a staple make-ahead recipe for use in Taco Salad Tilikum (page 73). You may also use the small red beans variation of the Precooked Soybeans recipe (page 161) if you don't want to use soy. *Note: This is very quick if you have the beans already made or use canned.

1¼ pounds lean ground beef
2 tablespoons dried minced onion
½ teaspoon garlic granules
2 teaspoons hot chili oil or about ¾ teaspoon cayenne
or chipotle pepper granules
1 teaspoon lemon pepper
½ teaspoon dried oregano
½ teaspoon ground cumin
½ teaspoon Sweet & Slender or SteviaPlus
2 teaspoons sea salt, divided
¼ cup water
2 tablespoons lard
4 cups Precooked Soybeans (page 161) or about 4 cans soybeans
2 teaspoons fresh-squeezed lime juice

1. Crumble the beef into a large saucepan; cook over medium heat, stirring constantly so that it is completely uniform in texture, until it is browned, about 4 to 5 minutes. Turn off the heat.
2. Drain the beef and return it to the pan. Add the dried onion, garlic granules, chili oil, lemon pepper, oregano, cumin, sweetener, 1 teaspoon of the salt, and the water stirring them well to combine. Continue to cook the meat until the water is mostly cooked out, about 2 minutes. Put the meat into a large dish, and set it aside.
3. In the same saucepan, warm the lard, beans, and remaining 1 teaspoon salt over medium-low heat. Using the back of a spoon or potato masher, mash most of the beans, but do not mash all of them. Pour the meat back into the saucepan along with the lime juice and stir until it is fairly well combined.

4. This may be kept refrigerated for up to 4 days or frozen into desired serving sizes in freezer bags for up to 1 month. To use frozen servings, thaw in the refrigerator and reheat on medium power in the microwave, stirring partway through.

Nutritional information per serving:
Carbohydrates: 6 grams; Effective Carb Count: 1 gram;
Protein: 18 grams; Fat: 20 grams; Calories: 272

Reduced-Fat Variation:
*Use extra-lean ground beef. In step 2, don't put the meat into a bowl.
Put the beans directly into the pan with the meat, omitting the lard.
Mash the beans while mixed with the meat.
Follow all remaining instructions as given.*
Carbohydrates: 6 grams; Effective Carb Count: 1 gram;
Protein: 19 grams; Fat: 15 grams; Calories: 232

BERRY MUSTARD GLAZED CHICKEN

Makes 18 servings

This delicious, mildly flavored chicken dish can also be done with boneless, skinless chicken on skewers "bento" style!

⅔ cup Bragg Liquid Aminos or light soy sauce
1 tablespoon sugar-free berry preserves
(raspberry, blackberry, or marionberry)
¾ teaspoon mustard powder
1 teaspoon SteviaPlus
1 tablespoon fresh-squeezed lemon juice
6 pounds fresh bone-in chicken or 4 pounds boneless

1. Combine the marinade ingredients in a small dish, mixing them well.
2. Place the chicken in a large shallow dish, such as a baking sheet that has a raised edge, and pour the marinade over the chicken. Allow the chicken to marinate, turning it frequently, for about 1 hour.
3. While the chicken is marinating, prepare your barbecue. Position the rack about 4 inches above the coals and heat the coals to about medium. Place the chicken on the rack and close the lid. Reserve the excess marinade to use as a basting sauce for the chicken while it is barbecuing. Pour the reserved marinade into a small saucepan and bring it to a boil over medium heat.
4. Barbecue the chicken, turning it frequently, for about 45 minutes. Baste the chicken often with the marinade. Close the lid of the barbecue between each turning/basting. The chicken will be firm to the touch and have a deep golden color when it is done. If you wish to test it with a meat thermometer, it should register at 180°F.
5. Store leftovers covered in the refrigerator for up to 4 days, or package individual portions in freezer bags for later use in lunches and for quick meals. Frozen portions may be kept frozen up to 1 month.

Nutritional information per serving:
Carbohydrates: 1 gram; Effective Carb Count: 0 grams;
Protein: 19 grams; Fat: 22 grams; Calories: 276

BREADING WITH A TWIST

Makes about 18 servings

This make-ahead breading recipe is incredibly versatile! It is delicious on fried okra, zucchini, and mushrooms. It can also be used for a delicious crunchy fish coating and for chicken nuggets. It makes enough mix to coat about 6 pounds of food.

4 cups crushed pork rinds
½ cup grated Parmesan cheese
1 tablespoon Old Bay Seasoning
2 teaspoons lemon pepper
2 tablespoons soy protein isolate

To use:
2 eggs
2 tablespoons water
Lard

1. Combine all of the breading ingredients in a plastic container with a lid. Shake well and store the breading mix in the refrigerator for up to 1 month.
2. To use the mix: Beat the eggs and water together in a shallow dish. Put some of the breading mix into another shallow dish. Dip the desired food into the egg mixture, then into the breading mixture, coating it evenly.
3. To cook the food, deep-fry it in a large wok or frying pan until golden brown. Alternatively, oven-fry it by greasing a baking sheet with about 2 or 3 tablespoons of melted lard. Arrange the breaded pieces on the sheet and bake at 375°F for about 25 minutes, until golden brown.

Nutritional information per serving (breading only):
Carbohydrates: trace; Effective Carb Count: 0 grams;
Protein: 11 grams; Fat: 11 grams; Calories: 133

BROCCOLI ALFREDO MINI-PIZZAS

Makes 2 servings

Is there anyone out there that always has leftover broccoli sitting in the fridge? Here's a yummy and different thing to do with it! If you have Alfredo sauce on hand, feel free to substitute it for the ranch.

2 (6") low-carb tortillas
Olive oil cooking oil spray
2 tablespoons Bacon Ranch Salad Dressing (page 60) or
commercially prepared ranch dressing
½ cup shredded Monterey jack cheese
½ cup chicken or pork, cooked and cubed
1 cup broccoli, chopped and cooked
2 tablespoons grated Parmesan cheese
Garlic salt, to taste
Dried basil, to taste

1. Preheat the oven to 400°F. Spray a baking sheet with cooking oil spray.
2. Place the tortillas on the baking sheet so that they aren't touching one another. Prebake for about 8 minutes, until just firm.
3. Layer the remaining ingredients on top of the tortillas in the order listed, reserving a bit of the Monterey jack to go on top of the broccoli with the Parmesan and garnishing each with a gentle sprinkling of the garlic salt and basil.
4. Bake for about 8 to 10 minutes, or until the cheese is melted and the pizzas are heated through.

Nutritional information per serving (chicken):
Carbohydrates: 15 grams; Effective Carb Count: 5 grams;
Protein: 26 grams; Fat: 25 grams; Calories: 357

Reduced-Fat Variation:
Use reduced-fat salad dressing and reduced-fat cheese. Spray the top of the pizzas with cooking spray before garnishing them with the garlic salt and basil. Follow all other instructions as given.
Carbohydrates: 16 grams; Effective Carb Count: 6 grams;
Protein: 26 grams; Fat: 14 grams; Calories: 275

Camarónes en Mojo de Ajo
(Mexican-Style Shrimp Scampi)

Makes 6 servings

A dear friend and I were treated to a lovely Mexican dinner. It was then that I experienced Mexican-style shrimp scampi for the first time. The lovely blend of seasonings tantalized my tongue! This recipe isn't a traditional scampi because prepeeling the shrimp is so time-consuming. Here we broil the shrimp in the shells and serve the sauce on the side. I think it is a lot more fun to peel the shrimp at the table than it is beforehand. If you can get the shell-off, uncooked shrimp, count yourself blessed and serve the sauce over the cooked shrimp. If you have extra sauce, it is excellent served over low-carb pasta or asparagus.

2 pounds raw shrimp, shells on (³¹⁄₄₀ size)
¾ cup butter
1 tablespoon olive oil
6 cloves garlic, minced
1 teaspoon red chili pepper flakes
1 tablespoon fresh-squeezed lime juice
1 teaspoon seasoning salt
1 cup sliced mushrooms

1. Place the shrimp into a large broiling pan or other broiler-safe pan. Broil the shrimp about 4" from the heat until the shells are pink, about 5 to 10 minutes.
2. Meanwhile, prepare the sauce. Put the butter, olive oil, and garlic into a medium-sized saucepan. Cook until the garlic is becoming translucent, about 3 minutes. Add the remaining ingredients in the order listed. Cook the sauce over medium-low heat for about 7 minutes or until the mushrooms are softened and the sauce is bubbly.
3. Serve the sauce in small bowls and allow guests to peel their shrimp and dunk them into it. Enjoy!

Nutritional information per serving:
Carbohydrates: 2 grams; Effective Carb Count: 2 grams;
Protein: 26 grams; Fat: 26 grams; Calories: 350

"CARNE" QUICK AND EASY

Makes 12 servings

Serve this as Tacos, Low-Carbed (page 177) or Enchiladas, Sharron-Style (page 135), or just eat it warm in a bowl topped with sour cream and salsa, if desired. Pork is the preferred, traditional preparation of this dish, but you can use just about any cut of meat you choose. This is a versatile recipe that always receives raves however it is prepared!

4 pounds boneless or 6 pounds bone-in meat,
(pork, beef, chicken, or turkey)
2 tablespoons garlic powder
2 tablespoons ground cumin
4 teaspoons seasoning salt
1½ teaspoons lemon pepper
½ teaspoon dried oregano
4 cups water
1 medium-sized onion, minced
2 teaspoons fresh-squeezed lime juice (fresh is always best!)
12 drops (about ½ teaspoon) hot chili oil
or about ¼ teaspoon cayenne pepper granules

1. Cut the meat into pieces that will easily fit into the pot. Place all of the ingredients *except* the lime juice and hot chili oil into a large pot with a lid. Bring it to a slow boil, then reduce the heat so it is just bubbling. Skim off any foam that rises to the surface. (These are impurities that will adversely affect the taste of your broth.) Be sure the meat remains completely covered in broth for the entire cooking time, adding more liquid if necessary.
2. Cook, covered, until the meat begins to fall off the bones, about 1½ hours for chicken and up to 4 hours for beef. Toward the end of the cooking time, add the lime juice and hot chili oil.

3. Transfer the pot to the refrigerator and allow it to cool until the fat rises to the top of the broth and becomes a hard layer; this usually takes overnight. Remove the fat (this also contains impurities that can affect the taste of the meat) and place the pot on the stove top; warm until the meat is workable. Remove the bones and other inedible parts and shred the meat, returning it to the broth so that it will stay moist.

4. To prepare the "Carne" in a slow cooker, place all of the ingredients *except* the lime juice and hot chili oil in the slow cooker. Cover and cook on low for about 10 hours, or on high for about 6 hours. Remove any foam that rises to the top. Toward the end of the cooking time, add the lime juice and chili oil. Follow the instructions for steps two and three.

Nutritional information per serving (using pork):
Carbohydrates: 4 grams; Effective Carb Count: 3 grams;
Protein: 22 grams; Fat: 29 grams; Calories: 368

Reduced-Fat Variation:
Use turkey instead of pork and follow the instructions given for removing the fat from the meat.
Carbohydrates: 4 grams; Effective Carb Count: 3 grams;
Protein: 31grams; Fat: 22 grams; Calories: 340

CHEESEBURGER CASSEROLE

Makes 8 servings

This is a yummy casserole that is great served for brunch as well as dinner. Enjoy the extras for lunch the next day or two. If you have access to bulk beef sausage, you can use it in place of the beef and seasonings. You can also skip the bread if you want! This is a very flexible recipe.

1 pound ground beef
½ medium-sized onion **or** 1 tablespoon dried minced onion
4 cloves garlic **or** 1 teaspoon garlic granules
2 slices low-carb bread, cut into ½" to 1" cubes
½ tablespoon olive oil
½ teaspoon ground sage
½ tablespoon dried parsley flakes
½ teaspoon dried rosemary
¼ teaspoon dried marjoram
8 drops hot chili oil (about ⅛ teaspoon) **or** a few grains of cayenne
½ teaspoon lemon pepper
1 tablespoon coconut oil **or** olive oil
½ tablespoon butter
½ teaspoon sea salt
1 teaspoon seasoning salt, divided
4 eggs
⅔ cup yogurt **or** kefir (sour cream could be used as well)
¾ cup shredded cheese (Cheddar, Colby, or a blend)
2 tablespoons grated Parmesan cheese
Basil, for garnish
Garlic granules, for garnish

1. Brown the beef, onions, and garlic in a frying pan over medium heat, about 6 to 8 minutes. Drain it.
2. Toss the bread cubes with the olive oil in a 9" x 13" baking pan. Bake in a 350°F oven for about 5 to 8 minutes, until they are nearly dry. Add the beef and seasonings (including ½ teaspoon of seasoning salt) to the baking dish and stir it well.
3. Combine the eggs, remaining ½ teaspoon of seasoning salt, and yogurt in a small dish, mixing well. Pour it over the bread and sausage mixture. Do not stir.
4. Sprinkle the cheeses over the top of the casserole. Garnish it with a very small amount of basil and garlic granules.
5. Bake the casserole for about 25 minutes at 350°F.
6. Refrigerate any leftovers and reheat in the microwave on medium power until they are warm.

Nutritional information per serving:
Carbohydrates: 3 grams; Effective Carb Count: 3 grams;
Protein: 18 grams; Fat: 22 grams; Calories: 286

Reduced-Fat Variation:
Use extra-lean ground beef and reduced-fat yogurt and cheeses. Follow all other instructions as given.
Carbohydrates: 3 grams; Effective Carb Count: 3 grams;
Protein: 19 grams; Fat: 16 grams; Calories: 244

CHEESEBURGER SOUP

Makes 8 servings

This delicious soup recipe was submitted by Connie Pritchett. It is really quick to prepare and seems to taste even better the second time around. It is a family favorite at our house, wonderful for those cold, snowy days!

1 pound lean ground beef
1 tablespoon coconut oil **or** lard
2 garlic cloves, minced
¾ cup chopped onion
¾ cup ¼" diced celery
½ cup shredded carrots (optional)
2 cups chopped chayote (also called mirliton) squash
or yellow summer squash
1 tablespoon fresh basil, chopped **or** 1 teaspoon dried
1 tablespoon fresh parsley, chopped **or** 1 teaspoon dried
3 cups beef Rich Stock (page 166) **or** commercially prepared beef broth
3 tablespoons butter
¼ cup soy protein isolate **or** vital wheat gluten flour
2 cups grated Cheddar cheese
1½ cups half-and-half
1 teaspoon sea salt
1 teaspoon ground black pepper **or** lemon pepper
½ cup sour cream
4 slices cooked bacon, chopped (optional)

>>

1. In a large saucepan brown the beef over medium heat. Drain off the grease and transfer the beef to a bowl; set it aside. In the same pan, melt the coconut oil and cook the veggies and the herbs until just tender, about 10 minutes.
2. Add the broth and the beef to the pot, and bring them to a low boil over medium heat. Reduce the heat and simmer the soup, covered, for about 20 minutes or until the veggies are nice and soft.
3. In a small frying pan, melt the butter over medium-low heat. Add the soy protein isolate and cook it, stirring frequently, until it is bubbling slightly. Add the mixture to the soup and bring to a low boil again. Cook it for about 2 minutes, stirring constantly.
4. Reduce the heat to low and add the cheese, half-and-half, salt, and pepper. Stir the soup until the cheese is melted.
5. Remove the pot from the heat and add the sour cream. Serve hot with bacon for garnish, if desired.

Nutritional information per serving:
Carbohydrates: 7 grams; Effective Carb Count: 5 grams;
Protein: 23 grams; Fat: 36 grams; Calories: 438

Reduced-Fat Variation:
Use reduced-fat cheese, fat-free half-and-half, low-fat sour cream, and turkey bacon. Follow all remaining instructions as given.
Carbohydrates: 11 grams; Effective Carb Count: 9 grams;
Protein: 24 grams; Fat: 20 grams; Calories: 325

CHICKEN SALAD BY THE BAY

Makes 4 servings

This is a superquickie recipe that can be made in about 5 minutes. It can be used to make Chicken Salad Sandwich Pizza Thingies (page 125) or just eaten out of the bowl with raw veggies! If you are using reduced-fat mayonnaise, be careful: It contains more carbs and sugar than the full-fat version.

2 (6.5-ounce) cans chicken (tuna can be substituted)
⅓ cup mayonnaise
1½ teaspoons dried minced onion
½ teaspoon Old Bay Seasoning
3 drops hot chili oil **or** *a few grains of cayenne pepper*
¼ teaspoon celery seeds

Place all the ingredients into a small bowl and mix well. Keep leftovers refrigerated for up to 3 days.

Nutritional information per serving:
Carbohydrates: 1 gram; Effective Carb Count: 1 gram;
Protein: 13 grams; Fat: 20 grams; Calories: 228

Reduced-Fat Variation:
Use reduced-fat mayonnaise. Follow all other instructions as given.
Carbohydrates: 4 grams; Effective Carb Count: 4 grams;
Protein: 12 grams; Fat: 8 grams; Calories: 143

CHICKEN SALAD SANDWICH PIZZA THINGIES

Makes 4 servings

These are so easy and so yummy! My kids often ask for them for lunch.

Coconut oil or lard (for the first method);
olive oil cooking spray (for the second method)
4 (6") low-carb tortillas
1 recipe Chicken Salad by the Bay (page 124)
8 ounces (about 2 cups) cheese, shredded
(Colby, Monterey jack, or a blend)
Dried basil

1. **First method:** For a crispy crust, heat about 1 teaspoon coconut oil in a medium-sized frying pan over medium heat until melted. Spread 1 tortilla with ¼ of the chicken salad and place it in the frying pan. Sprinkle with ¼ of the cheese and a gentle sprinkling of basil. Cook until the cheese melts, about 5 minutes. Repeat with the remaining tortillas. Serve hot.
2. **Second method:** If you are in a hurry and don't mind the crust being less crisp, spread out all of the tortillas on a baking sheet that has been sprayed with cooking oil spray. Prepare as described above. Bake at 350°F for about 8 minutes, until the cheese is melted. Serve hot.

Nutritional information per serving (first method):
Carbohydrates: 13 grams; Effective Carb Count: 4 grams;
Protein: 32 grams; Fat: 44 grams; Calories: 539

Reduced-Fat Variation:
Use the reduced-fat variation of the Chicken Salad by the Bay (page 124) and reduced-fat cheese. Follow the second cooking method.
Carbohydrates: 18 grams; Effective Carb Count: 9 grams;
Protein: 33 grams; Fat: 16 grams; Calories: 343

CONEY DOGS

Makes 8 servings

When I was a little girl, my mother used to take me to the local drive-in where we would share a "shrimp boat"—a basket of fries and fried shrimp. Later, when I started growing and half of a meal would not satisfy me, my mother changed our menu items to Coney Dogs. I still love them piled high with chili and cheese, low-carbed, of course!

1 pound all-beef franks, nitrate-free, if possible
½ recipe Seven Hill's Chili with Beans (page 168)
1 cup shredded Cheddar cheese

Optional toppings:
½ cup finely chopped sweet onion
1 (4-ounce) can sliced jalapeños
1 (4-ounce) can sliced black olives
½ cup sour cream

1. Boil, broil, or pan-fry the franks until hot. Place each into a bowl or onto a plate with a deep rim.
2. Divide the chili then the cheese atop the franks. Serve at the table with the optional toppings of your choice. Eat them with a knife and fork and lots of napkins!

Nutritional information per serving
(optional toppings not included):
Carbohydrates: 6 grams; Effective Carb Count: 4 grams;
Protein: 19 grams; Fat: 31 grams; Calories: 378

Reduced-Fat Variation:
Use reduced-fat Seven Hill's Chili with Beans (page 169)
and reduced-fat franks, cheese, and sour cream.
Follow all remaining instructions as given.
Carbohydrates: 6 grams; Effective Carb Count: 3 grams;
Protein: 19 grams; Fat: 23 grams; Calories: 310

EASY BEEF AND GREEN BEANS

Serves 6

One day I was smoking a salmon, but I had a lot of trouble getting the smoker up to the correct temperature. The salmon was taking way too long, and my kids were all looking at me with pitiful faces. I had compassion for them, so I fixed this. Their pitiful faces turned into smiling faces! If you use leftover Easy-Peasy Greeny Beanies (page 81), then you'll want to decrease the seasoning amounts.

1¼ pounds lean ground beef
3 cloves garlic, minced
2 cups chopped celery
1 (16-ounce) bag frozen green beans, cut or whole
1 cup mushrooms, sliced
1 teaspoon seasoning salt
½ teaspoon lemon pepper
2 tablespoons Bragg Liquid Aminos or soy sauce
1 teaspoon sesame oil
¼ teaspoon hot chili oil or about ⅛ teaspoon cayenne
or chipotle pepper granules

1. Brown the ground beef along with the garlic over medium heat until the red is gone from the meat, about 5 minutes.
2. Add the veggies and cook until softened, about 15 minutes.
3. Add the remaining ingredients and stir well. Serve this quick meal in bowls.

Nutritional information per serving:
Carbohydrates: 8 grams; Effective Carb Count: 5 grams;
Protein: 19 grams; Fat: 21 grams; Calories: 300

EASY CHICKEN CORDON BLEU

Makes 12 servings

Sometimes even the busiest of us need to entertain! This meal is so very simple to prepare and is impressive when served. It only takes about 45 minutes from start to finish. Simple, fast, and delicious—a sure winner! If your chicken pieces are large, you will have to allow for more coating and longer cooking time. Be sure and use that meat thermometer. You can use breasts, but they will require a toothpick to hold them together.

1 egg
1 tablespoon water
¾ cup almonds, finely ground
1½ teaspoons seasoning salt
½ teaspoon dried parsley flakes
12 boneless, skinless chicken thighs (approximately 2¾ pounds)
¼ pound Swiss cheese, cut into 12 slices
⅓ pound deli-style ham, cut into 12 slices
Cooking oil spray

1. Combine the egg and water in a bowl large enough to dip the chicken. Combine the almonds, seasoning salt, and parsley in another bowl, about the same size. Divide the cheese and ham into 12 pieces each.
2. Place a chicken thigh onto a plate, cut-side up. Place a piece of the cheese into the center of the chicken. Roll up a piece of ham and place it on top of the cheese. Roll the chicken up around the ham and cheese.
3. Dip the rolled chicken first into the egg mixture, then into the almond mixture. Carefully place the chicken, seam-side down, onto a baking sheet that has been sprayed with cooking oil spray. Repeat with the remaining thighs.
4. Bake the chicken at 350°F for 25 minutes or until the chicken is firm to the touch or tests at 180° with a meat thermometer.

Nutritional information per serving:
Carbohydrates: 2 grams; Effective Carb Count: 1 gram;
Protein: 15 grams; Fat: 11 grams; Calories: 160

Easy "Deli" Lunchmeat

Makes about 16 servings

I use this recipe to make my husband lunchmeat that doesn't have all the nitrates and other stuff in it that we don't want to put in our bodies. Sure, I could make it fancier and use lots of herbs, etc., but why? This is so easy and so good! Once you have mastered the method, have fun experimenting with a variety of seasonings and spices.

2½–3 pounds boneless pork roast or turkey breast
Seasoning salt
Lemon pepper

1. Liberally season all sides of the meat with the seasoning salt and lemon pepper.
2. Pour about ¼ cup water into a roaster. Place the meat in the roaster and cover it with a lid. (If you don't have a covered baking pan, use a fairly deep pan and tightly cover it with foil while baking.) Bake it at 350°F for about 1½ hours or until the meat reaches 180°F on a meat thermometer.
3. Cool the meat at room temperature until it is easy to handle. Wrap it thoroughly with plastic wrap and refrigerate it overnight.
4. Remove the meat from the refrigerator and slice it with a very sharp knife to desired thickness. Place the slices into containers and freeze the extras for up to 1 month.

Nutritional information per serving:
Carbohydrates: 0 grams; Effective Carb Count: 0 grams;
Protein: 13 grams; Fat: 12 grams; Calories: 161

Reduced-Fat Variation:
Use the turkey breast instead of the pork roast.
Follow all other instructions as given.
Carbohydrates: 0 grams; Effective Carb Count: 0 grams;
Protein: 14 grams; Fat: 4 grams; Calories: 100

EASY HAM "N" BEANS

Makes 8 large servings

Beans? But we can't have beans on a low-carb diet! Calm down. These are soybeans. They are higher in protein and lower in carbohydrates than other legumes. This recipe isn't for induction levels, but it is useful for an occasional treat while on ongoing weight loss. For a real Southern-style treat, serve them overcooked collard greens. If you don't want to use soybeans, you can use the small red beans variation of the Precooked Soybeans recipe (page 161).

1 medium-sized onion, chopped
4 cloves garlic, minced (about 1½ tablespoons)
1 small carrot, cut up (optional)
1 bunch celery, ends and tops only, chopped (about 1 cup)
Approximately 5 cups water, divided (filtered preferred)
1 meaty hambone or hock; or 2 cups cubed ham; or 1 pound cooked bacon, chopped
4 cups Precooked Soybeans (page 161) or the equivalent canned
½ teaspoon thyme flakes
1–1½ teaspoons sea salt
¼ teaspoon lemon pepper
1–1½ tablespoons butter
3 tablespoons vital wheat gluten flour or soy protein isolate

1. Put the onion, garlic, carrot, and celery into a large soup pot with 2 cups of the water. Cover the pot and bring it to a boil. Reduce it to a rapid simmer for about 10 minutes or until the veggies are beginning to soften.
2. Add the hambone, soybeans, thyme, and enough water to cover the hambone, about 3 cups. Cover the pot and bring it to a boil, then reduce to a rapid simmer for about 1 hour or until all the ingredients are tender.

3. Remove the hambone from the pot and chop the meat. Return it to the pot and add the salt and lemon pepper.
4. Melt the butter in a small pan over medium heat. Stir in the vital wheat gluten and stir well. Cook it for about 1 or 2 minutes, until it bubbles rapidly and begins to break up, then add it to the soup and stir well.
5. Alternate cooking method: Place the veggies, meat, beans, and thyme into a slow cooker and add enough water to cover all the ingredients. Cook the soup on low heat all day, about 6 to 8 hours. Follow the remaining instructions.
6. This soup may be kept in the refrigerator for up to 4 days or frozen for up to a month.

Nutritional information per serving:
Carbohydrates: 10 grams; Effective Carb Count: 3 grams; Protein: 21 grams; Fat: 9 grams; Calories: 199

Reduced-Fat Variation:
Use lean ham and omit the butter and vital wheat gluten. Follow all other instructions as given.
Carbohydrates: 10 grams; Effective Carb Count: 3 grams; Protein: 17 grams; Fat: 7 grams; Calories: 164

EASY LEMON PEPPER CHICKEN

Makes 4 servings

You don't have to use just boneless chicken. In fact, I have been known to purchase the family packs of just "whatever" chicken pieces and cook up to 15 pounds of this at a time when we've had family gatherings or just needed food precooked for a busy week. Just be sure to allow for extra cooking time. One friend of mine said of this dish, "It's better than my favorite restaurant's best chicken!"

1½ tablespoons lard
1¼ pounds boneless, skinless chicken, legs or breasts
Seasoning salt
Lemon pepper

1. Melt the lard in a large frying pan over medium heat. Season the chicken well on one side with the seasoning salt and lemon pepper. Place the chicken into the pan seasoned-side down. Liberally season the side that is face-up with seasoning salt and lemon pepper.
2. Cook the chicken until it begins to brown on the first side, then turn it over and brown the other side. Continue cooking and turning it as needed until it is done, about 35 minutes or until it tests at 180°F (170°F for breasts) with a meat thermometer.

Nutritional information per serving:
Carbohydrates: 0 grams; Effective Carb Count: 0 grams;
Protein: 16 grams; Fat: 8 grams; Calories: 139

EASY POT ROAST AND VEGGIES

Makes 10 servings

This isn't necessarily "quick" but it sure is simple, and delicious, too! This is a great "now and later" recipe. Cook it up ahead of time and you'll have an easy meal ready to go when you are.

Lard **or** coconut oil
4½-pound boneless beef chuck roast
Lemon pepper
Seasoning salt
1¼ cups beef Rich Stock (page 166) or commercially prepared broth
1 bunch celery, cut into 4" pieces
1 small head cauliflower, cut into 2" chunks
1 sweet onion, cut into 8 pieces
4 carrots, cut into 4" pieces (optional)
Approximately 1 teaspoon xanthan gum or arrowroot

1. Place about 1 to 2 tablespoons of the lard into the bottom of a large frying pan or in the bottom of your roasting pan if it is stovetop safe. Melt over medium heat.
2. Season the roast liberally on all sides with seasoning salt and lemon pepper while the lard is melting. Once the lard is melted, place the roast in the hot pan and brown it on all sides, about 3 or 4 minutes total.
3. Place the roast into a roaster with a cover and pour the stock into the bottom of the pan. (If you are using frozen stock as directed in the Rich Stock [page 167] recipe, it is not necessary to thaw it.) Alternatively, you can cook the roast and veggies in a slow cooker for about 8 to 12 hours on low.
4. Cover the pan and bake it at 325°F for about 45 minutes. Add the veggies and cook for about another 1 to 1½ hours, or until the roast is tender.
5. Remove the roast and veggies to a serving dish. Slice the roast thinly so it can be used as sandwiches, wraps, etc.

6. Pour the broth from the roast into a small saucepan and bring it to a simmer over medium heat. Gently sprinkle the xanthan gum over the bubbling broth. (Sprinkle it very lightly or you will end up with clumps.) Whisking constantly, heat the gravy until it thickens to the desired consistency, adding more xanthan gum if necessary. Serve the gravy over the meat and veggies.

Nutritional information per serving:
Carbohydrates: 5 grams; Effective Carb Count: 3 grams;
Protein: 33 grams; Fat: 33 grams; Calories: 459

ENCHILADAS, SHARRON-STYLE

Makes 12 servings

This is a wonderfully special meal! It is great for company, but is also a great choice for lunches from "planned-overs."

½ prepared recipe of "Carne" Quick and Easy (page 118)
12 (6") low-carb tortillas or small corn tortillas
¾ pound Monterey jack cheese, shredded

1. If the "Carne" is cold, heat it until steaming. Spoon just enough of the broth from the "Carne" to cover the bottom of a 9" x 13" baking dish. Preheat oven to 350°F.
2. Place about ½ to 1 cup of the steaming broth into another shallow dish that has a curved edge. Dip the tortillas one at a time into the warm broth to soften them. Keep the broth warm by adding fresh broth as the tortillas are soaking.
3. Place a softened tortilla on a plate or other work surface and fill with about ⅓ to ½ cup of the prepared meat. Roll up the tortilla, overlapping the sides and leaving the ends open; place seam-side down in the baking dish. Continue in this fashion until all of the enchiladas are assembled. (If the tortillas break while you are rolling them, that is okay; they will bake just fine.)
4. Cover the enchiladas with the cheese. Bake for about 25 minutes or until the cheese melts and becomes golden in places.
5. Package up any leftovers in sealable freezer bags for use in lunches. They can be frozen for up to 1 month.
6. To reheat the enchiladas, remove them from the bag and place on a microwave-safe plate; warm medium power in the microwave until hot.

Nutritional information per serving:
Carbohydrates: 14 grams; Effective Carb Count: 4 grams;
Protein: 28 grams; Fat: 22 grams; Calories: 338

Reduced-Fat Variation:
Use reduced-fat cheese and follow all other directions as given.
Carbohydrates: 15 grams; Effective Carb Count: 5 grams;
Protein: 28 grams; Fat: 15 grams; Calories: 281

FAKE-ARONI AND CHEESE CASSEROLE

Makes 12 servings

Think of that timeless, kids' favorite macaroni and cheese and you've got the idea! This casserole can be used as the base for many variations. You can put the cheese on top instead of inside. You can use just about any meat or fish. If you use fish, use ½ to 1 teaspoon dill weed instead of paprika. Cauliflower works best, but you can also use cabbage cut into strips or chopped broccoli for the veggie base.

3 cups sour cream
4 eggs
2½ cups shredded cheese
(Colby, Monterey jack, Cheddar, mozzarella, etc.)
½ teaspoon paprika
3 tablespoons dried minced onion
2 teaspoons seasoning salt
½ teaspoon lemon pepper
2 pounds cauliflower, chopped into ½" pieces (approximately 8 cups, either fresh or frozen)
2 pounds beef franks, cut into bite-sized pieces
Olive oil cooking spray
2 tablespoons parsley flakes

1. In a large mixing bowl, stir together the sour cream, eggs, cheese, and all the spices (*except* the parsley) thoroughly with a wire whisk. Stir the cauliflower and franks into the cheese mixture.
2. Spray a 9" x 13" x 2" pan with cooking oil spray and pour ½ of the cauliflower and cheese mixture into the pan. Spread the mixture evenly and sprinkle it with ½ of the parsley flakes. Bake it at 350°F for about 25 to 35 minutes, or until it is bubbly and golden.

3. Pour the remaining cauliflower mixture into another baking pan (not glass!) that has been completely lined with foil. Sprinkle it with the remaining parsley flakes. Place it in the freezer. Freeze until solid, then gently remove the casserole in the foil from the pan. Discard the foil and wrap the casserole completely with plastic wrap. The casserole can be frozen for up to 1 month.

4. To bake the frozen casserole, remove the plastic wrap. Return the casserole to the baking pan and cover the top with foil. Bake at 325°F for about 35 minutes, then remove the foil and allow it to continue baking until it is heated through, about 50 to 60 minutes.

Nutritional information per serving:
Carbohydrates: 8 grams; Effective Carb Count: 6 grams;
Protein: 18 grams; Fat: 38 grams; Calories: 440

Reduced-Fat Variation:
Use chicken hot dogs, low-fat sour cream, and reduced-fat cheese. Follow all remaining instructions as given.
Carbohydrates: 12 grams; Effective Carb Count: 10 grams;
Protein: 19 grams; Fat: 18 grams; Calories: 284

FRIED PRAWNS

Makes 4 servings

This was a recipe born of opportunity! One strategy I use to make my life simpler is to precook a whole bunch of meat at the same time. On the day this recipe was born, I made Easy "Deli" Lunchmeat (page 129), Easy Lemon Pepper Chicken (page 132), and some Ranch Chops (page 164). This gives us already-prepared food for many days, and I don't have to think about it again for a while. I just threw the shrimp into the fat from the Easy Lemon Pepper Chicken (page 132). What a treat!

Bacon grease and lard, for frying
1½ pounds raw shrimp or prawns, shells on

1. Heat about ½" of bacon grease and lard combined in a large frying pan until it is hot.
2. Carefully place the shrimp into the hot fat and cook them on each side until they are dark pink in color, about 3 minutes total.
3. Serve with Lemon Butter (page 86), Bacon Ranch Salad Dressing (page 60), or another sauce of your choice. Allow guests to peel the shrimp themselves at the table.

Nutritional information per serving:
Carbohydrates: 0 grams; Effective Carb Count: 0 grams;
Protein: 28 grams; Fat: 14 grams; Calories: 246

GREAT GRANDMA'S GERMAN SAUSAGE BAKE

Makes 8 servings

We went to visit Great Grandma. She said, "I've been meaning to tell you of a recipe that my children always asked me to make. It was a family favorite!"

2½ pounds bulk pork sausage
2 pounds frozen cauliflower
4 ounces (½ cup) cream cheese, softened
1 tablespoon butter
½ teaspoon seasoning salt
2 cans sauerkraut (about 2 pounds), drained
½ tablespoon dried parsley flakes

1. Cook the sausage on medium heat until it is no longer pink. Drain any excess fat.
2. Meanwhile, cook the cauliflower in a covered pot with about 1" water until it is soft, about 10 minutes. Drain it and mash the cauliflower with a potato masher. Mash in the cream cheese, butter, and seasoning salt until well combined.
3. Spread the sausage in an even layer in the bottom of a 9" x 13" baking pan. Layer the sauerkraut on top, then spread the mashed cauliflower with the back of a spoon. Sprinkle the top with the parsley flakes.
4. Bake it at 350°F for about 25 to 30 minutes or until the top begins to turn golden.

Nutritional information per serving:
Carbohydrates: 7 grams; Effective Carb Count: 3 grams; Protein: 19 grams; Fat: 25 grams; Calories: 324

Reduced-Fat Variation:
Use turkey sausage, reduced-fat cream cheese, and omit the butter.
Follow all other instructions as given.
Carbohydrates: 7 grams; Effective Carb Count: 3 grams; Protein: 19 grams; Fat: 9 grams; Calories: 186

GREEN AND WHITE SAUCE WITH LOW-CARB PASTA

Makes 6 servings

This delicious sauce can be used over low-carb pasta, Rice-Aflower (page 92) or Slurp 'Em Up Cabbage Noodles (page 95). Who could turn down this scrumptious dish as a next-day lunch? Trina Nelson, a professional chef, came up with these yummy variations: 1. Add 1 cup sliced mushrooms to the pan while cooking the garlic; 2. Use 2 tablespoons chopped fresh basil instead of the parsley.

6 ounces low-carb pasta (I use Bella Vita Low-Carb Cavatappi)
6 cloves garlic, minced
2 tablespoons olive oil
1 bunch spinach, washed and trimmed of stems (about 3 cups total)
3 cups chicken, cooked and cubed
1½ teaspoons seasoning salt
¾ teaspoon lemon pepper
¾ cup half-and-half or cream
⅓ cup shredded Parmesan cheese, plus extra for garnish
½ cup chopped fresh parsley or ¼ cup dried parsley flakes

1. Cook the pasta according to the package directions.
2. While the pasta is cooking, sauté the garlic in the olive oil over medium heat in a medium-sized saucepan until softened, about 2 minutes.
3. Add the spinach and cook, stirring constantly, until wilted, about 2 minutes.
4. Add the chicken, seasoning salt, and lemon pepper; cook until the chicken is heated through, stirring throughout.
5. Turn off the heat and add the half-and-half, the ⅓ cup Parmesan cheese, and the parsley.
6. Pour the sauce and cooked pasta into a serving dish and toss well. Serve with extra Parmesan cheese.

>>

Nutritional information per serving:
Carbohydrates: 13 grams; Effective Carb Count: 8 grams;
Protein: 28 grams; Fat: 20 grams; Calories: 323

Reduced-Fat Variation:
Instead of the half-and-half, use canned skim milk.
Follow all remaining instructions as given.
Carbohydrates: 15 grams; Effective Carb Count: 10 grams;
Protein: 30 grams; Fat: 16 grams; Calories: 309

GREEN, WHITE, AND RED SAUCE WITH LOW-CARB PASTA

Makes 6 servings

This terrific variation on the Green and White Sauce with Low-Carb Pasta (page 140) was developed by Trina Nelson, a professional chef, during the testing process for this cookbook. We thought it was so good that it deserved its own recipe! You can serve this over Slurp 'Em Up Cabbage Noodles (page 95) or Rice-Aflower (page 92) instead of low-carb pasta, if you desire.

6 ounces low-carb pasta (I use Bella Vita Low-Carb Cavatappi)
4 slices bacon, chopped (without nitrates, if possible)
1 tablespoon olive oil
6 cloves garlic, minced
1 bunch spinach, washed and trimmed of stems (about 3 cups total)
3 cups cubed chicken, cooked
1½ teaspoons seasoning salt
¾ teaspoon lemon pepper
¾ cup half-and-half or cream
⅓ cup shredded Parmesan cheese, plus extra for garnish
¼ cup dried parsley flakes or ½ cup chopped fresh parsley

1. Cook the pasta according to the package directions.
2. While the pasta is cooking, cook the bacon in the olive oil over medium heat in a medium-sized saucepan until it is just becoming crisp, about 4 minutes. Transfer the bacon to a small dish, leaving the drippings in the pan.
3. Cook the garlic in the pan drippings over medium heat until softened, about 2 minutes.
4. Add the spinach and cook it, stirring constantly, until wilted, about 2 minutes.
5. Add the chicken, seasoning salt, and lemon pepper; cook until the chicken is heated through, stirring constantly.

6. Turn off the heat and add the half-and-half, ⅓ cup Parmesan cheese, and parsley.
7. Pour the sauce and cooked pasta into a serving dish and toss them well. Serve with extra Parmesan cheese.

Nutritional information per serving:

Carbohydrates: 13 grams; Effective Carb Count: 8 grams;
Protein: 30 grams; Fat: 19 grams; Calories: 328

Reduced-Fat Variation:

Use canned skim milk and turkey bacon.
Follow all remaining instructions as given.
Carbohydrates: 15 grams; Effective Carb Count: 10 grams;
Protein: 31 grams; Fat: 16 grams; Calories: 312

ITALIAN DRESSING CHOPS

Makes 8 servings

I always keep a bottle of Bernstein's Italian Dressing with Cheese on hand for times when I have no time or energy to do something more involved with my pork chops. If you don't have Bernstein's available, even the cheapest store-bought Italian dressing will do nicely. This recipe also works well on the grill.

8 meaty pork chops
⅔ cup bottled Italian salad dressing (Bernstein's preferred)

1. If you have time, marinate the chops in a large plastic sealable bag with the salad dressing for 30 minutes up to overnight. If you don't have time, just skip to the next step.
2. Place the chops in a large baking pan. Pour the salad dressing over the chops. Bake them at 400°F for about 25 to 35 minutes, until they test at 170°F on a meat thermometer.
3. Keep leftovers covered in the refrigerator.

Nutritional information per serving:
Carbohydrates: 2 grams; Effective Carb Count: 2 grams;
Protein: 23 grams; Fat: 24 grams; Calories: 323

Reduced-Fat Variation:
Use reduced-fat salad dressing. Follow all other instructions as given.
Carbohydrates: 2 grams; Effective Carb Count: 2 grams;
Protein: 23 grams; Fat: 17 grams; Calories: 253

Kraut Doggies

Makes 4 servings

This is a grown-up version of Piggies in Blankets (page 156). It is messy to eat, so be prepared with lots of napkins!

4 (6") low-carb tortillas
½ cup shredded cheese (Monterey jack, Colby, Cheddar, or a blend)
4 bratwurst sausages, cooked
½ cup sauerkraut
1 tablespoon lard or coconut oil

1. Heat a large frying pan or griddle over medium temperature. Warm the tortillas and place them on a cutting board or plate.
2. Sprinkle ¼ of the cheese down the center of each tortilla, then place a bratwurst on top of the cheese. Top them with ¼ of the sauerkraut. Roll the tortilla up and set aside, flap-side down. Repeat with the remaining tortillas.
3. Melt the lard in the griddle over medium heat. Place the wrapped dogs in the pan, flap-side down, being very careful not to burn your fingers. Cook, turning only once in the direction in which they are wrapped, until golden brown, about 3 minutes total. Serve hot.

Nutritional information per serving:
Carbohydrates: 14 grams; Effective Carb Count: 4 grams; Protein: 15 grams; Fat: 21 grams; Calories: 275

Reduced-Fat Variation:
Use turkey or chicken sausages, reduced-fat cheese, and olive oil cooking spray. Follow all remaining instructions as given.
Carbohydrates: 14 grams; Effective Carb Count: 4 grams; Protein: 16 grams; Fat: 11 grams; Calories: 202

Lamb Riblets

Makes 6 servings

We so enjoy lamb at my home. We don't get it very often because of the expense, but every so often it goes on sale. I don't even have to tell my kids when I'm cooking it—they can smell it before I even say anything! This marinade can be used for any lamb that is suitable for grilling or broiling. It is particularly yummy with broiled lamb chops. What could be easier than grilling some meat and having it later?

3 pounds lamb riblets
2–3 cups Rich Stock, any flavor (page 166) or commercially prepared
2 tablespoons fresh-squeezed lemon juice
¼ teaspoon ground cinnamon
1 teaspoon garlic granules, roasted if available
1½ teaspoons seasoning salt
1 teaspoon lemon pepper
¼ teaspoon ground ginger
½ teaspoon hot chili oil or about ¼ teaspoon cayenne
or chipotle pepper granules

1. Cut the lamb riblets into equal-sized pieces, if necessary.
2. Combine the marinade ingredients in a large container with a lid. Put the meat into the marinade, and cover the container. Refrigerate for about 2 hours, up to overnight.
3. Before grilling, remove the meat from the marinade and sprinkle it with some additional lemon pepper. Grill it to medium-rare or medium, 130°F to 145°F.

Nutritional information per serving:
Carbohydrates: 1 gram; Effective Carb Count: 1 gram;
Protein: 22 grams; Fat: 29 grams; Calories: 356

MEAT LOAF MANIA!

Makes about 12 servings

Make 1 of these babies for now and the other for later. Eat the leftovers as sandwiches on low-carb bread or crackers or cut it up and put it into a yummy omelette. Instead of the Bacon Ranch Salad Dressing (page 60), you could use Pizza Sauce (page 158) or Mock Cream of Mushroom Soup (page 89) for a nice topping.

1¼ pounds ground pork
1¼ pounds lean ground beef
⅓ cup half-and-half or cream
¾ cup ground pork rinds
2 eggs
½ teaspoon hot chili oil or a pinch of cayenne
1½ teaspoons seasoning salt
1 teaspoon lemon pepper
1 teaspoon ground sage
3 tablespoons dried minced onion
4 tablespoons dried parsley flakes, divided
1 teaspoon mustard powder
¼ teaspoon SteviaPlus or 1 packet sucralose
⅓ cup Bacon Ranch Salad Dressing (page 60)

1. In a large mixing bowl with an electric mixer, combine all the ingredients *except* the salad dressing and 1 tablespoon parsley. Mix on low speed until thoroughly combined.
2. Divide the meat loaf mixture in half. Wrap 1 portion completely in plastic wrap and place in the freezer for up to 1 month. Place the other half into a loaf pan, about 9" x 4" x 4." Bake it at 350°F for approximately 1 hour.
3. Remove the meat loaf from the oven and use a spoon to scoop any excess grease from the top. Spread the salad dressing evenly on top and sprinkle it with the remaining parsley. Bake for 15 to 20 minutes.

Nutritional information per serving:
Carbohydrates: 2 grams; Effective Carb Count: 2 grams;
Protein: 20 grams; Fat: 28 grams; Calories: 339

Reduced-Fat Variation:
*Use ground chicken or turkey instead of the pork and
canned skim milk instead of the half-and-half.
Follow all remaining instructions as given.*
Carbohydrates: 3 grams; Effective Carb Count: 3 grams;
Protein: 21 grams; Fat: 21 grams; Calories: 282

MEXICAN PIZZAS

Makes 4 servings

You could also use the Seven Hill's Chili with Beans (page 168) recipe as a base, or the "Carne" Quick and Easy (page 118) would work, as well. Be creative!

Cooking oil spray
4 (6") low-carb tortillas
1 cup Taco Meat (page 176)
1 (4-ounce) can sliced black olives
1 cup shredded cheese (a Mexican blend would be perfect)
¼ cup sour cream

Topping choices:
1 (4-ounce) can black olives, sliced
1 medium-sized tomato, chopped
Salsa
Chopped fresh cilantro
¼ cup chopped onion
1 (4-ounce) can sliced jalapeño peppers, sliced

1. Spray a large baking sheet with cooking oil spray.
2. Place the tortillas on the baking sheet so that the tortillas aren't touching one another. Divide the meat evenly between the tortillas. Top with the olives and then the cheese.
3. Bake them at 375°F for about 10 minutes or until the cheese is melted.
4. Remove the tortillas from the oven and cut them into halves or fourths, if desired. Top with the sour cream and the toppings of your choice.
5. Have lots of napkins ready!

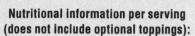

**Nutritional information per serving
(does not include optional toppings):**
Carbohydrates: 13 grams; Effective Carb Count: 4 grams;
Protein: 23 grams; Fat: 26 grams; Calories: 355

Reduced-Fat Variation:
*Use reduced-fat sour cream, reduced-fat cheese,
and the reduced-fat variation of Taco Meat (page 176).
Follow all remaining instructions as given.*
Carbohydrates: 13 grams; Effective Carb Count: 4 grams;
Protein: 22 grams; Fat: 16 grams; Calories: 264

OVEN-FRIED CHICKEN

Makes 6 servings

This simple make-ahead recipe is delicious served by itself or with any number of the sauces in this book baked on it after the frying step. If you have leftover breading after making the chicken, you can dip onion slices, cut-up okra, zucchini, or mushrooms into the buttermilk then the breading mix as described below and fry them in the hot fat for a yummy appetizer while you are waiting on the chicken! To make the chicken extra moist and tender, marinate it in commercial chicken stock infused with herbs for 30 minutes up to overnight.

Breading Ingredients:
½ cup vital wheat gluten flour
½ cup milk and egg protein powder
2 teaspoons seasoning salt
1 teaspoon lemon pepper
½ teaspoon paprika

Other ingredients:
½ cup buttermilk or kefir
4 pounds chicken pieces
Lard, for frying

1. Combine the breading ingredients in a shallow dish. Put the buttermilk into another shallow dish. Dip the chicken first into the buttermilk, then dredge the chicken in the gluten mixture. Place the dredged pieces into a large baking pan while you finish this step. You may need to prepare additional breading, depending upon the size of your chicken pieces.
2. Heat the lard in a large frying pan over medium heat. Place the dredged chicken pieces into the hot fat, skin-side down. Allow it to brown lightly, then turn and continue to cook it, about 15 minutes total.

3. Place the browned chicken into a large baking dish and, if using a sauce, divide it evenly over the tops of the chicken. Bake it at 375°F for about 40 to 50 minutes or until it tests at 180°F and the chicken is golden and crunchy.
4. If you want to prepare this as a make-ahead for the freezer, after step 2, place the chicken on baking sheets and freeze them. When they are frozen solid, put them into zippered storage bags, and freeze them up to one month.
5. To prepare the frozen chicken, bake them at 375°F for about an hour, or until they test at 180°F.

Nutritional information per serving:

Carbohydrates: 3 grams; Effective Carb Count: 3 grams;
Protein: 31 grams; Fat: 20 grams; Calories: 317

PARTY WRAPS

Makes 12 servings

You can make these ahead of time to use for lunches and quick meals during the week, or, as the name suggests, take them to your next get-together!

12 (6") low-carb tortillas
1 cup Spinach Dip (page 206) or commercially prepared
2 pounds deli-style lunchmeat, very thinly sliced

1. Place a tortilla on a plate or cutting board and spread about 1 tablespoon of the dip onto half of the tortilla.
2. Divide the lunchmeat into 12 equal portions. Place one portion onto the half of the tortilla that has the dip.
3. Roll up the tortilla, meat-side first. The fillings will slide and the whole wrap will be filled when it is rolled.
4. Cut the wrap in half and either place it onto a serving plate or into a large plastic zippered bag. Repeat with the remaining ingredients.

Nutritional information per serving:
Carbohydrates: 18 grams; Effective Carb Count: 9 grams;
Protein: 20 grams; Fat: 11 grams; Calories: 217

Reduced-Fat Variation:
Use reduced-fat spinach dip.
Follow all remaining instructions as given.
Carbohydrates: 18 grams; Effective Carb Count: 9 grams;
Protein: 19 grams; Fat: 2 grams; Calories: 166

PASTA AND SAUSAGE WITH HEART

Makes 8 servings

This is so fast and so delicious! You can have this on the table in 20 minutes, if your meat is precooked. This is also wonderful made with 3 cups cooked, cubed chicken.

6 ounces low-carb pasta (I use Bella Vita Low-Carb Cavatappi)
¼ cup olive oil
1 tablespoon butter
⅔ cup Rich Stock, any flavor (page 166) or commercially prepared broth
1 pound bratwurst or Italian sausage, cooked
1 (4-ounce) can mushrooms, sliced, drained
1 (6-ounce) can sliced black olives, drained
1 teaspoon dried rosemary
1 tablespoon dried parsley flakes
½ teaspoon garlic granules
1 teaspoon lemon pepper
1 teaspoon (or up to 1 tablespoon, according to taste) red wine vinegar
1 (14-ounce) can artichoke hearts, drained

1. Cook the pasta according to package directions; drain it.
2. Meanwhile, warm the butter, olive oil, and stock in a medium-sized saucepan over medium heat until the butter melts. Add the meat, mushrooms, olives, and seasonings; cook until warmed through, stirring.
3. Put the artichoke hearts into the bottom of a large serving bowl. Pour the sauce over them and toss them gently. Add the pasta and combine it well with the sauce. Serve hot.

Nutritional information per serving:
Carbohydrates: 16 grams; Effective Carb Count: 9 grams;
Protein: 21 grams; Fat: 26 grams; Calories: 359

Reduced-Fat Variation:
Use turkey bratwurst instead of regular.
Follow all remaining instructions as given.
Carbohydrates: 15 grams; Effective Carb Count: 8 grams;
Protein: 23 grams; Fat: 16 grams. Calories: 272

PEANUT BUTTER CHICKEN

Makes 6 servings

I had a family-sized package of legs/thighs and I didn't know what to do with them. I was inspired to create this delicious sauce with an Asian flair! When you pack it for lunch, just be sure to take lots of napkins! This delicious sauce can also be used as a dipping sauce for Shake It and Bake It! chicken (page 170) or Breading with a Twist chicken (page 115).

1 recipe Oven-Fried Chicken (page 151)
½ cup peanut butter
1 teaspoon SteviaPlus
¼ cup Bragg Liquid Aminos or soy sauce
1 tablespoon sesame oil
¼ teaspoon hot chili oil or about ⅛ teaspoon cayenne
or chipotle pepper granules
1 teaspoon ground ginger
1 teaspoon garlic granules
½ medium-sized onion, finely chopped
¾ cup (or more, if necessary) coconut milk

1. Prepare the meat as instructed in steps 1 and 2 of the Oven-Fried Chicken recipe (page 151).
2. While the chicken is frying on the stovetop, place all of the sauce ingredients into a small saucepan. Simmer them on low heat until they begin to thicken. If the sauce becomes too thick, add more coconut milk.
3. Place the browned chicken into a large baking dish and divide the sauce evenly over the tops of the chicken. Bake it at 350°F for about 1 hour, or until it tests at 180°F.

Nutritional information per serving (sauce only):
Carbohydrates: 7 grams; Effective Carb Count: 5 grams;
Protein: 6 grams; Fat: 21 grams; Calories: 224

PIGGIES IN BLANKETS

Makes 4 servings

This quick and easy meal is a kid-friendly favorite. If at all possible, try to get hot dogs that don't contain nitrates and preservatives, which are available at many natural food stores. You can make this simple treat into party fare by slicing them up and serving them with Sweet-and-Zingy Mustard Sauce (page 173) and other sauces from this book, or your own creations. Put out a bowl of toothpicks and let your guests have fun!

4 (6") low-carb tortillas
½ cup shredded cheese (Monterey jack, Colby, Cheddar, or a blend)
4 hot dogs
1 tablespoon lard or coconut oil

1. Heat a large frying pan or griddle over medium temperature. Warm the tortillas and place them on a cutting board or plate.
2. Sprinkle ¼ of the cheese down the center of each tortilla, then place a hot dog on top of each. Roll up the tortillas, letting them sit flap-side down for about 1 minute.
3. Melt the lard on the griddle and place the wrapped hot dogs on it, flaps down, being very careful not to burn your fingers. Cook for about 3 minutes, turning the dogs periodically so that all sides are evenly golden. Serve hot.

Nutritional information per serving:
Carbohydrates: 14 grams; Effective Carb Count: 5 grams;
Protein: 15 grams; Fat: 26 grams; Calories: 324

Reduced-Fat Variation:
Use reduced-fat cheese and turkey or chicken hot dogs.
Follow all other instructions as given.
Carbohydrates: 13 grams; Effective Carb Count: 4 grams;
Protein: 15 grams; Fat: 15 grams; Calories: 225

PIZZA BURGERS

Makes 2

Sometimes I open up my refrigerator and look into it blankly. It stares at me blankly. We stare at each other for a while. Then I ask it, "What am I going to eat?" This was the reply on one such occasion! Seriously, if you can't decide between burgers and pizza, why decide? Have them both at the same time!

2 (¼-pound) lean hamburger patties (fresh or frozen)
1 tablespoon Pizza Sauce (page 158) or commercially prepared sauce
(just watch the carb count!)
4 slices pepperoni
⅓ cup shredded mozzarella cheese

1. Cook the hamburger patties over medium heat in a frying pan until they are about medium-well done, turning once. They should start to feel firm, but not hard. While the patties are cooking, warm the pepperoni in the same pan to release some of the excess grease.
2. Divide the pizza sauce between the two patties. Top them with the pepperoni and cheese.
3. Turn off the heat and cover the pan. Let sit, covered, for 1 or 2 minutes to allow the cheese to melt. The total cooking time will be about 6 minutes, if using thawed hamburger, a little longer if using frozen. Serve hot.

Nutritional Information per serving:
Carbohydrates: 2 grams; Effective Carb Count: 2 grams;
Protein: 21 grams; Fat: 26 grams; Calories: 331

Reduced-Fat Variation:
Use extra-lean ground beef and reduced-fat cheese. Spray the pan with cooking oil spray if necessary during cooking to prevent sticking. Follow all remaining instructions as given.
Carbohydrates: 2 grams; Effective Carb Count: 2 grams;
Protein: 24 grams; Fat: 21 grams; Calories: 297

PIZZA SAUCE

Makes about 4 servings

This is my sister's tried-and-true recipe for from-scratch pizza sauce. It is delicious! You can use it as a dipping sauce or as a quick and easy sauce for low-carb pasta.

1 (8-ounce) can tomato sauce (roasted garlic flavored is nice!)
1 teaspoon Italian seasoning (the combination used contains basil,
sweet marjoram, parsley, garlic, and red pepper flakes)
¼ cup finely chopped onion or 1 tablespoon dried minced onion
1 bay leaf
¼ teaspoon seasoning salt or sea salt
Tiny pinch SteviaPlus or sucralose

In a small saucepan, combine all the ingredients. Simmer for 15 minutes. Remove from the heat and allow the sauce to cool completely.

Nutritional information per serving:
Carbohydrates: 5 grams; Effective Carb Count: 4 grams;
Protein: 1 gram; Fat: 0 grams; Calories: 22

POUNDED PATTIES

Makes about 12 servings

My momma made these when I was a little girl. She would really hammer on the meat. I think she did it to get her frustrations out! I just tap the "flour" into the meat. I love how the meat gets so tender. This is a great make-ahead meal. The patties can be used for sandwiches on low-carb bread or crackers, rolled up in low-carb tortillas, or just warmed and eaten as is. They are even great for breakfast with fried eggs on the side. My favorite accompaniments to serve with these are Mock Cream of Mushroom Soup (page 89) and Cauli Mash (page 78).

3 pounds lean ground beef
Approximately 2 cups soy protein isolate or vital wheat gluten flour
Olive oil cooking spray, for frying
Seasoning salt
Lemon pepper (optional)

1. Divide the meat into balls between ⅛ pound and ¼ pound in size.
2. Place a dinner plate in front of you and put a generous amount of soy protein isolate on the plate. Put 1 of the meatballs on the plate. Sprinkle the top of the ball with some of the soy protein isolate and press it down flat. Continue pressing and adding protein powder until the patty is very thin and really won't hold any more of the powder.
3. As you complete the patties, stack them onto another dinner plate, sprinkling additional protein powder on the plate and between each patty. You will also need to layer waxed paper between them, especially if you are using wheat gluten, to keep them from sticking together.

4. When you are done pressing out the patties, spray the cooking oil spray in a large frying pan. Place the patties into the frying pan one at a time, so they are just touching. Sprinkle the tops with seasoning salt and lemon pepper and cook them until they are just browned on each side, spraying additional cooking oil spray as necessary. Transfer the patties to a platter. The patties can be kept warm in the oven, set at the lowest temperature, if you are feeding a crowd.
5. Serve with your choice of sauces. Refrigerate or freeze any leftovers.

Nutritional information per serving:
Carbohydrates: 0 grams; Effective Carb Count: 0 grams;
Protein: 35 grams; Fat: 24 grams; Calories: 373

PRECOOKED SOYBEANS

Makes 12 servings

Soybeans are a bit fussier than other dried legumes. You cannot add any of the seasonings or other ingredients until they have been mostly cooked, or they will toughen. They also take a bit longer to soak. That said, this is a very simple recipe that is a building block for several others in this book. Feel free to double or triple this recipe and freeze the precooked beans in sealable plastic bags for later use. If you don't want to use soybeans, simply follow the recipe and replace the soybeans with small red beans. Small red beans have a total higher carb count, but the effective carb count is actually less!

2 cups (1 pound) dried soybeans (available at most health food stores)
12 cups water (filtered preferred), divided

1. In a large covered pot, soak the beans in 6 cups of water at room temperature for 6 to 8 hours or overnight. Remove any floating or shriveled beans and debris.
2. Drain and rinse the beans. Return them to the pot with the remaining 6 cups of water. Do not salt the beans.
3. Bring the beans to a boil over medium-high heat with the pot loosely covered, so that the steam can escape. Reduce the heat to a simmer and continue to cook the beans for about 3 hours, until they are tender. Alternatively, they may be cooked in a slow cooker for about 8 hours on low heat.
4. The cooked beans may be kept refrigerated for up to 1 week or frozen for about 1 month.

Nutritional information per serving (soybeans):
Carbohydrates: 12 grams; Effective Carb Count: 8 grams;
Protein: 14 grams; Fat: 8 grams; Calories: 164

Nutritional information per serving (small red beans):
Carbohydrates: 25 grams; Effective Carb Count: 7 grams;
Protein: 9 grams; Fat: 0 grams; Calories: 66

QUICK AND EASY CREAM GRAVY

Makes about 8 to 12 servings

This recipe is useful for just about any gravy purpose, although my favorite is when I make Easy "Deli" Lunchmeat (page 129). I take the bits and pieces of roast that didn't slice nicely and the defatted broth from the roast, and I make a lovely gravy to serve over Rice-Aflower (page 92) or low-carb toast. One friend of mine likes to use the chicken version as a base for her homemade chicken soup.

4–6 cups broth, pan drippings, or Rich Stock (page 166)
4–6 ounces cream cheese
Salt, to taste
Black pepper or lemon pepper, to taste

1. If the pan drippings are chilled, defat them by peeling or scraping the fatty layer off of the top. Pour the drippings and any additional stock, if needed into a saucepan. Heat it over medium heat until it boils.
2. Place the cream cheese in a microwave-safe container big enough to mix the cream cheese with some broth after it is warmed. Microwave until it is very soft, about 30 to 45 seconds. Beat the softened cream cheese with a wire whisk or fork until smooth.
3. Carefully remove about ¼ cup of the boiling stock from the pan with a measuring cup or ladle, and add it to the cream cheese. Whisk it until it is smooth, then pour the cream cheese mixture into the bubbling broth. Stir until it is uniform in texture. Add the seasonings, to taste. (I find after I cook a roast and use only the pan drippings that I need to add very little in the way of seasonings—it is usually just perfect as it is!)

Nutritional information per serving:
Carbohydrates: 0 grams; Effective Carb Count: 0 grams;
Protein: 1 gram; Fat: 5 grams; Calories: 49

Reduced-Fat Variation:
Use reduced-fat cream cheese. Follow all other instructions as given.
Carbohydrates: 0 grams; Effective Carb Count: 0 grams;
Protein: 1 gram; Fat: 3 grams; Calories: 37

RANCH CHICKEN

8 servings

I get precut chicken whenever possible! I usually buy the legs and thighs that are still hooked together, or the packages called "the best of the fryer." Then, all I have to do is rinse the chicken pieces and season them. This recipe also works on the barbecue quite nicely.

8 pieces chicken
⅓–½ package ranch salad dressing mix
1 teaspoon lemon pepper

1. Rinse the chicken under running water. Shake off the excess water into the sink or pat the pieces dry with paper towels.
2. Place the chicken into a large baking pan and season it with the ranch mix and lemon pepper. Bake it for about 45 minutes at 375°F or until the chicken tests at 180°F on a meat thermometer.

Nutritional information per serving:
Carbohydrates: 1 gram; Effective Carb Count: 1 gram;
Protein: 16 grams; Fat: 14 grams; Calories: 204

Reduced-Fat Variation:
Remove the skin from the chicken before baking.
Follow all remaining instructions as given.
Carbohydrates: 1 gram; Effective Carb Count: 1 gram;
Protein: 8 grams; Fat: 3 grams; Calories: 69

RANCH CHOPS

Serves 8

This is so easy! Make a batch even on a busy night and you'll have food for a couple of days.

8 pork chops
⅓–½ package ranch salad dressing mix
1 teaspoon lemon pepper

1. Rinse the chops under cold running water, shake off excess water, and place them onto a baking sheet. Sprinkle the tops of the chops with the ranch mix and lemon pepper.
2. Bake them for about 20 minutes at 400°F or until they are becoming golden or test at 170°F on a meat thermometer. You may also broil the chops, but be wary of splatters!

Nutritional information per serving:
Carbohydrates: 1 gram; Effective Carb Count: 0 grams;
Protein: 23 grams; Fat: 15 grams; Calories: 237

REFRIED SOYBEANS

Makes 8 servings

Most Mexican food is the ultimate in quick and easy. It is simple, straightforward, and delicious. However, the low-carb lifestyle doesn't permit many of the old favorites. Recently, though, I've discovered substitutions for many of my old favorites! Serve these with Tacos, Low-Carbed (page 177) or as a yummy dip for Low-Carb Tortilla Chips (page 194). If you don't want to use soybeans, you can follow the small red beans variation of the Precooked Soybeans recipe (page 161).

1½ tablespoons lard
2 (15-ounce) cans Eden Organic Black Soybeans, drained and juices reserved, or 2 cups Precooked Soybeans (page 161)
1 teaspoon dried minced onion
½ teaspoon garlic granules
¾ teaspoon seasoning salt
A few drops hot chili oil or a few grains of cayenne pepper granules

1. Warm the lard in a large skillet over medium-low heat and add the beans. Mash about ½ to ⅔ of the beans with a potato masher or the back of a wooden spoon. (Do not mash all of the beans; leaving some of them whole adds texture.)
2. Add the seasonings and some of the reserved juices from the beans to keep them from sticking to the pan. Heat them through, stirring constantly. Serve hot.

Nutritional information per serving:
Carbohydrates: 4 grams; Effective Carb Count: 1 gram;
Protein: 5 grams; Fat: 5 grams; Calories: 78

Reduced-Fat Variation:
Omit the lard. Use extra bean juices as necessary. Follow all remaining instructions as given.
Carbohydrates: 4 grams; Effective Carb Count: 1 gram;
Protein: 5 grams; Fat: 3 grams; Calories: 57

RICH STOCK

Makes about 2 gallons total

This is one of my "basic kitchen necessity" recipes. I use it nearly every day, and it is a basic component for many of my soups and stews. It is also essential for Sharron's Beef Jerky (page 202), which I consider a mainstay of my diet! I usually make this after dinner with the bones, fat, and skin left from the meal. I then allow it to cook all night on a back burner of my stove. I waken to yummy smells in the morning and my tummy is usually growling!

2 tablespoons lard, if making beef or pork stock
Approximately ¾ pound beef or pork fat/trimmings and bones (the bones are really important!) or 1 chicken or turkey carcass, meat removed, leaving only skin and bones
1 onion, peeled
2 carrots, peeled
2 large ribs celery
2 cloves garlic, peeled
2 bay leaves
1 teaspoon peppercorns, whole (optional)
Salt

1. If making beef or pork stock, place the lard into a 5- to 9-quart stockpot and brown the fat, meat trimmings, and bones over medium heat. If making chicken or turkey stock, skip this step and just add the carcass as is to the stockpot.
2. Cut the onion, carrots, and celery in half. Add them to the stockpot along with the garlic and bay leaves. Add enough water to the pot to fill it to 3 inches below the rim. Cover the pot and bring it to a boil. Lower the heat until it is simmering very slowly, and cook it for about 12 hours. Alternatively, it may be cooked in a slow cooker on low heat for about the same amount of time.

>>

3. While this is simmering, a lot of foam and debris will come to the top. These are the impurities coming out of the stock. Remove them with a spoon and discard. The end result will be a wonderfully flavored, clear stock!

4. When the stock is a rich, golden color, it can be removed from the heat, salted to taste, and allowed to cool. Alternatively, if a reduced, more intensely flavored stock is desired, remove the lid, increase the heat, and bring the stock back to a slow boil. Continue to boil the stock until it has cooked down ⅓ to ½ its original volume. (How much you reduce the stock will depend upon how intense you want the flavor of the stock to be.) Add salt to taste.

5. Allow the stock to cool thoroughly, then strain it. Pour it into clean ice cube trays and freeze. After the stock has frozen, it can be placed into freezer containers or zippered freezer bags and stored for several months.

6. To use: Remove as much stock as is needed and thaw for use in recipes requiring broth.

Nutritional information per serving:
Carbohydrates: 0 grams; Effective Carb Count: 0 grams;
Protein: 0 grams; Fat: 0 grams; Calories: 0

Q M

SEVEN HILL'S CHILI WITH BEANS

Serves 8

Put this in a slow cooker first thing in the morning and you'll come home to wonderful smells in the evening. Freeze half of it and you'll have a tasty treat for another day! This is a great part of Coney Dogs (page 126).

1 pound ground pork
1 pound ground beef (coarse ground for chili, if possible)
2 tablespoons dried minced onions
1 tablespoon garlic granules
3 bay leaves
Salt and pepper, to taste
3–4 tablespoons chili powder
1 teaspoon dried oregano
2 teaspoons ground cumin
2 (14–16 ounce) cans chopped tomatoes (without sugar)
½ red bell pepper, finely chopped
2 (8-ounce) cans tomato sauce
2 (15-ounce) cans Eden Organic Black Soybeans, drained, or 2 cups Precooked Soybeans (page 161)
½–1 cup water, depending on how thick you want the chili
2 tablespoons chopped fresh parsley

1. In a large skillet with a lid, cook the pork and beef over medium heat until it is no longer red. Drain off grease.
2. Add the remaining ingredients *except* the parsley to the pan and mix well. If using a slow cooker, put everything into it and mix well.
3. Cover and simmer over medium-low heat for 30 minutes. If using a slow cooker, cook it on low for about 6 to 8 hours, or on high for 4 to 6 hours.
4. Stir the parsley into the chili and let it simmer an additional 5 minutes.

>>

Nutritional information per serving:
Carbohydrates: 9 grams; Effective Carb Count: 5 grams;
Protein: 17 grams; Fat: 20 grams; Calories: 285

Reduced-Fat Variation:
Substitute ground turkey for the pork and use extra-lean ground beef.
Follow all remaining instructions as given.
Carbohydrates: 9 grams; Effective Carb Count: 4 grams;
Protein: 18 grams; Fat: 12 grams; Calories: 214

Q
M

SHAKE IT AND BAKE IT!

Makes 24 servings

Here's a great quickie meal. Just ½ cup of mix is enough to coat approximately 2 pounds of meat. It makes excellent chicken or pork nuggets as well as chops or breaded baked chicken. Try different salad dressing mixes and enjoy a variety of flavors. Just watch out for sugar in the salad dressing mixes!

2 cups crushed pork rinds
2 packets ranch salad dressing mix
¼ cup soy protein isolate

1. Combine the ingredients and place them into an airtight container. Store the mix for up to 1 month.
2. When you are ready to use the mix, place the desired amount of mix and meat into a large plastic bag and shake it until the meat is well coated. Bake the meat at 400°F until desired doneness is reached, about 10 minutes for nuggets and up to 20 or 30 minutes for chops.

Nutritional information per serving:
Carbohydrates: 1 gram; Effective Carb Count: 0 grams;
Protein: 4 grams; Fat: 3 grams; Calories: 48

SMOKED SALMON, THE EASY WAY

Makes 8 to 12 servings

This isn't a fancy smoked fish recipe, but the results are fantastic! It is so easy! You don't have to use salmon, but whatever fish you choose should have the skins on, or it will fall apart in the smoking process.

2 large salmon fillets
Sea salt
Old Bay Seasoning

1. Liberally salt the salmon and place it into a container with a lid. Cover and refrigerate it for up to 3 days.
2. When you have time to do the smoking process, take the salmon out of the refrigerator and place it into the sink, while still in the container.
3. Rinse the fish very well, changing the water several times.
4. Place the fish onto a large baking sheet and season it liberally with the Old Bay Seasoning. Place it into a hot smoker and smoke it according to the manufacturer's directions.
5. Keep the fish refrigerated for up to 1 week or freeze it in serving-size portions in freezer bags for later use.

Nutritional information per serving (3 ounces, cooked):
Carbohydrates: 0 grams; Effective Carb Count: 0 grams; Protein: 22 grams; Fat: 11 grams; Calories: 196

SWEET-AND-SOUR SAUCE, TAKE TWO

Yields about 6 servings

My husband and I were asked to create a program using a dinner and a movie theme. The movie the folks wanted us to use was about a lady who went to the Philippines. I learned the original version of this great recipe while I was preparing myself to do those dinners. Now it is not only quick and easy like the original, but it is also low-carb! Serve as a dipping sauce or use as a basting sauce for chicken or pork. It is great on Basic Ribs (page 109).

¼ cup cider or wine vinegar (red or white)
¾ teaspoon SteviaPlus
3 packets sucralose
1 teaspoon sea salt
2 tablespoons tomato sauce
1½ cups water
½ teaspoon xanthan gum
½ cup pineapple chunks (optional)
2 tablespoons chopped bell pepper (optional)
2 tablespoons chopped tomato (optional)

1. Combine the vinegar, SteviaPlus, sucralose, salt, tomato sauce, and water in a small saucepan; bring to boil over medium heat.
2. Gently sprinkle the xanthan gum over the sauce while it is boiling. Let it boil briefly, stirring until the sauce thickens and there are no lumps.
3. Use as a dipping sauce or baking sauce. Add the optional ingredients, if desired, when baking. The sauce may be covered and refrigerated for up to 2 weeks.

Nutritional information per serving:
Carbohydrates: 1 gram; Effective Carb Count: 1 gram;
Protein: 0 grams; Fat: 0 grams; Calories: 4

SWEET-AND-ZINGY MUSTARD SAUCE

Makes 8 servings

This sauce is a great dip for burgers, hot dogs, pork, chicken or whatever! It even makes a nice addition to plain ol' chicken or tuna salad with mayo.

2 tablespoons mustard powder
½ teaspoon ground ginger
¼ teaspoon lemon pepper
2 packets sucralose
⅛ teaspoon chipotle pepper granules or ¹⁄₁₆ teaspoon cayenne
1 tablespoon Bragg Liquid Aminos or soy sauce
2 tablespoons water

Combine all ingredients in a small dish. Serve as a dipping sauce. Cover and refrigerate any leftovers for up to 1 week.

Nutritional information per serving:
Carbohydrates: 0 grams; Effective Carb Count: 0 grams;
Protein: 0 grams; Fat: 0 grams; Calories: 6

TACO CASSEROLE

Makes 8 servings

This yummy dinner pie can be used just as easily for breakfast or brunch as it can for dinner. Don't hesitate to add different toppings or try variations. This is an easy winner!

8 eggs
⅓ cup kefir or buttermilk
2 tablespoons milk and egg protein powder
½ teaspoon dried cilantro or 1 teaspoon chopped fresh cilantro
¼ teaspoon dried oregano
1/16 teaspoon chipotle pepper granules or hot chili oil
1 teaspoon seasoning salt
¾ cup shredded cheese (Cheddar, Colby, or a blend)
¾ cup Taco Meat (page 176)
Olive oil cooking spray

Toppings:
½ cup sour cream
½ cup shredded cheese (Cheddar, Colby, or a blend)
½ cup sliced olives
½ cup salsa, fresh tomatoes, or both

1. In a mixing bowl, combine the eggs, buttermilk, protein powder, and seasonings with a wire whisk. Add the cheese and taco meat, mixing well.
2. Spray a 10" pie pan with cooking oil spray. Pour the casserole mixture into the pie pan.
3. Bake the casserole at 325°F for about 35 to 40 minutes or until a knife inserted just off center comes out clean.
4. Spread the sour cream over the finished pie and add the remaining toppings. Slice it and serve!
5. Store leftovers covered in the refrigerator. Reheat in the microwave on medium power until warm.

Nutritional information per serving:
Carbohydrates: 2 grams; Effective Carb Count: 1 gram;
Protein: 11 grams; Fat: 13 grams; Calories: 174

Reduced-Fat Variation:
Use reduced-fat kefir, cheese, and sour cream. Follow the reduced-fat variation of the Taco Meat (page 176) recipe. Follow all remaining instructions as given.
Carbohydrates: 2 grams; Effective Carb Count: 2 grams;
Protein: 13 grams; Fat: 10 grams; Calories: 154

TACO MEAT

Makes about 6 servings

I like to keep a batch of this made up for quick lunches and dinners. It is great in Taco Casserole (page 174) and several other recipes in this book.

1½ pounds ground beef
½ medium onion, chopped
2 cloves garlic, minced
2 tablespoons butter
¼ cup water
2 teaspoons hot chili oil or about 1 teaspoon cayenne
or chipotle pepper granules
1 teaspoon lemon pepper
½ teaspoon dried oregano
1 teaspoon sea salt
½ teaspoon ground cumin
½ teaspoon Sweet & Slender or SteviaPlus

In a large skillet, brown the ground beef and drain it in a large colander. While the beef is draining, cook the onions and garlic in the butter until becoming golden, about 5 minutes. Add the beef and remaining ingredients. Simmer until most of the moisture has evaporated, about 5 minutes. This may be kept refrigerated up to 3 days or frozen for up to 1 month.

Nutritional information per serving:
Carbohydrates: 2 grams; Effective Carb Count: 1 gram;
Protein: 19 grams; Fat: 36 grams; Calories: 409

Reduced-Fat Variation:
Use lean ground beef and cook the onion and garlic along with the beef.
Follow all the remaining instructions as given.
Carbohydrates: 2 grams; Effective Carb Count: 1 gram;
Protein: 20 grams; Fat: 25 grams; Calories: 323

TACOS, LOW-CARBED

Makes about 10 servings

Even with low-carb tortillas, these really should be considered a treat. Enjoy them loaded up with all your favorite fillings! If you have everything ready to go, you can just warm the meat and tortillas, and you've got an easy already-made dinner. You can also use "Carne" Quick and Easy (page 118), Refried Soybeans (page 165), or Beef and Refried Beans (page 112) as a filling for your tacos. Quick and Easy Lemon Pepper Chicken (page 132) would also be a good filling choice.

1 recipe Taco Meat (page 176)
10 (6") low-carb tortillas
4 cups shredded lettuce
1 cup shredded cheese (Cheddar or Colby)

Additional topping choices:
Simply Guacamole (page 204)
Refried Soybeans (page 165)
Sour cream
Black olives, sliced
Tomato, chopped
Salsa

1. Heat the Taco Meat (page 176) to serving temperature, if necessary.
2. Warm the tortillas one at a time on a medium-hot dry griddle or frying pan. Flip them once, for a total cooking time of about 30 seconds each. Alternatively, you wrap them in a slightly dampened cloth and warm them in the microwave for about 10 to 15 seconds. (Be very careful, as they will get rubbery quickly if overheated in the microwave!)
3. Let each person fill the tortillas as desired, and serve them with lots of napkins!

Nutritional information per serving:
Carbohydrates: 13 grams; Effective Carb Count: 4 grams;
Protein: 20 grams; Fat: 20 grams; Calories: 289

Reduced-Fat Variation:
*Use the reduced-fat variation of the Taco Meat (page 176) recipe
and reduced-fat cheese. Follow all remaining instructions as given.*
Carbohydrates: 13 grams; Effective Carb Count: 4 grams;
Protein: 21 grams; Fat: 14 grams; Calories: 243

TARTAR SAUCE

Makes 6 servings

This quicky recipe is always a winner! Every time I serve it to guests, they ask for the recipe. Serve with fish, chicken, or pork.

⅓ cup mayonnaise
1½ teaspoons dried minced onion
1 teaspoon fresh-squeezed lemon juice
¼ teaspoon dill weed
⅛ teaspoon lemon pepper

Combine all of the ingredients and mix well. Store in a covered container in the refrigerator for up to 2 weeks.

Nutritional information per serving:
Carbohydrates: 0 grams; Effective Carb Count: 0 grams;
Protein: 0 grams; Fat: 10 grams; Calories: 89

Reduced-Fat Variation:
Use reduced-fat mayonnaise and follow all other instructions as given.
Carbohydrates: 2 grams; Effective Carb Count: 1 gram;
Protein: 0 grams; Fat: 3 grams; Calories: 32

Q
M

TERIYAKI BEEF

Makes 12 servings

You can have your teriyaki sauce and eat it, too. This simple sugar-free recipe adds a delicious kick to beef. It can be used on chicken and pork, as well.

3 pounds boneless beef sirloin steak or roast
½ cup Bragg Liquid Aminos or soy sauce
2 teaspoons ground ginger
⅛ teaspoon roasted chipotle pepper granules or hot chili oil
2 tablespoons garlic granules (roasted, if available)
1 teaspoon SteviaPlus
4 packets sucralose
½ teaspoon lemon pepper

1. Slice the beef into strips ½" thick by about 3" to 4" long. Place them in a large plastic container with a lid.
2. Combine the remaining ingredients in a small dish. Pour them over the beef strips and stir well. Cover and marinate the meat for about 20 minutes.
3. Discard the marinade, and broil or barbecue the meat until done, about 8 minutes.

Nutritional information per serving:
Carbohydrates: 1 gram; Effective Carb Count: 1 gram;
Protein: 21 grams; Fat: 16 grams; Calories: 240

TRINA'S PIZZA CRUST

Makes 8 servings

This wonderful crust, developed by a professional chef, will make a delicious addition to your low-carb way of eating! Instead of making 1 big pizza, you can separate the crust mixture into 3 portions and make individual-sized pizza crusts that can be frozen for later use. Just bake them as directed in step 4, let them cool, and freeze them in plastic wrap. Thaw them for a few minutes before adding toppings and baking as instructed in step 5.

3 eggs, at room temperature
3 tablespoons whole-milk ricotta cheese
1 teaspoon garlic powder
½ teaspoon salt
1 tablespoon grated Parmesan cheese
1 cup shredded mozzarella cheese
Olive oil cooking spray or butter

1. Preheat the oven to 325°F. Separate the egg whites from the yolks. Place the whites into a mixing bowl, and set them aside.
2. Place the yolks into a blender with the ricotta, garlic powder, and salt. Blend the yolk mixture until it is smooth.
3. Meanwhile, beat the egg whites until stiff peaks form. Fold the yolk mixture, Parmesan, and mozzarella cheeses into the whites.
4. Spray or butter a 12" pizza pan. Spread the mixture evenly onto the pan. Bake it for 45 to 50 minutes, until it is firm and browned.
5. While the crust is still hot, add Pizza Sauce (page 158), Bacon Ranch Salad Dressing (page 60), or your favorite sauce, cheese, and the toppings of your choice. Return the pizza to the oven for about 5 minutes, until the cheese has melted. Let it rest at room temperature for a few minutes before slicing and serving.

Nutritional information per serving:
Carbohydrates: 1 gram; Effective Carb Count: 1 gram;
Protein: 6 grams; Fat: 6 grams; Calories: 84

Reduced-Fat Variation:
Use part–skim ricotta and mozzarella cheeses.
Follow all remaining instructions as given.
Carbohydrates: 1 gram; Effective Carb Count: 1 gram;
Protein: 7 grams; Fat: 5 grams; Calories: 76

WONTON SOUP WITHOUT THE WONTONS

Makes 6 servings

We went to a delightful little Chinese restaurant. We wandered into the restaurant, searching for a pay phone, but came back because of the wonderful smells! They served a wonderful Wonton Soup. I skipped the dumplings and enjoyed the delicious vegetables and meats. Theirs had shrimp and pork. You may certainly use those, but this is what I had on hand when I made mine. I actually used the juices and bits and pieces left from a couple of roasted chickens for the base of my soup. Feel free to vary the meats and veggies. Be creative and enjoy!

2 stalks celery, cut into ½" dice
1 medium-sized carrot, (optional)
1 cup broccoli, cut into 1" chunks
½ cup green beans
1 small yellow summer squash, diced (about 1 cup)
1½ cups diced cooked chicken
3/4 teaspoon seasoning salt
4–6 cups chicken-based Rich Stock (page 166) or
commercially prepared chicken broth
2 cups baby spinach leaves or washed, torn spinach
2 eggs

1. Place all of the ingredients *except* the spinach and eggs into a medium-sized saucepan, adding enough stock to cover the veggies. Cover the pan and bring it to a boil.; Reduce it to a simmer until the veggies are just tender, about 10 minutes.
2. In a small bowl, beat the eggs with a fork until they are frothy. Set them aside.
3. Add the spinach to the soup and stir to mix. Gently pour the egg mixture over the soup. Allow it to rest for a few seconds before stirring the egg in 1 direction *only*. Serve hot. Freeze any leftovers or use within 3 days.

Nutritional information per serving:
Carbohydrates: 3 grams; Effective Carb Count: 1 gram;
Protein: 2grams; Fat: 4 grams; Calories: 135

5

Snacks
and Treats

CANDIED ALMONDS

Makes 16 ½-cup servings

This fun recipe can be used to make many different flavors of nuts. You can use caramel sauce on peanuts and it will taste like the peanuts out of a Cracker Jack box! The results are only limited to your flavors of syrups and your imagination. Try combining syrups for new flavors. Be bold and experiment. You'll never know what you can come up with until you try! These are a great on-the-go snack.

1½ teaspoons coconut oil or butter
2 tablespoons sugar-free specialty syrup (the kind for coffee)
1 pound (approximately 4 cups) raw almonds
2 teaspoons SteviaPlus
⅛ teaspoon sea salt (optional)
Olive oil cooking spray

1. Preheat oven to 350°F.
2. Place the coconut oil into a microwave-safe bowl large enough to hold all of the ingredients. Microwave the coconut oil on high power for about 1 minute, or until it is melted.
3. Stir the syrup into the melted oil and add the nuts, mixing well. Add the SteviaPlus (and sea salt), and mix it well.
4. Pour the coated nuts onto a baking sheet that has been sprayed with cooking oil spray, scraping the bowl well and spreading the nuts evenly over the sheet.
5. Bake the nuts for about 15 minutes, stirring them once during baking. Pour them at once into a heat-safe container, scraping any of the caramelized bits off the pan and into the bowl. Allow them to cool completely for best flavor and crunch.

Nutritional information per serving:
Carbohydrates: 6 grams; Effective Carb Count: 3 grams;
Protein: 6 grams; Fat: 15 grams; Calories: 171

CHEESE STICKS

Makes 8 servings

Keep these in the fridge for quick afternoon snacks. Just warm them slightly in the microwave and dip them in Pizza Sauce (page 158), if desired.

1 cup ground pork rinds
2½ tablespoons soy protein isolate
¼ teaspoon lemon pepper (optional, if grownups are eating these too!)
1 teaspoon Italian seasoning (optional)
1 egg
8 ounces mozzarella "string cheese," cut into 16 pieces
1 tablespoon water
¼ cup lard

1. Combine the pork rinds, soy protein isolate, and lemon pepper in a shallow dish. In another shallow dish, combine the egg and water.
2. Melt the lard in a medium-sized frying pan over medium heat.
3. Meanwhile, dip the cheese sticks first into the egg-water mixture, then into the pork rind mixture. Fry them over medium heat, turning often, until brown. Serve warm.

Nutritional information per serving:
Carbohydrates: 1 gram; Effective Carb Count: 0 grams;
Protein: 9 grams; Fat: 14 grams; Calories: 158

CINNAMON TARTS

Makes 4 servings

When I was a little girl and my mommy made pies, she always seemed to have pie dough left over. She would spread it with butter, cinnamon, and sugar, and bake it for a special treat. These aren't just for childhood, though! I've come up with a low-carb version for every kid at heart.

4 packets sucralose
½ teaspoon SteviaPlus
½ teaspoon ground cinnamon
3 (6") low-carb tortillas
3 teaspoons butter

1. Combine the sweeteners and cinnamon in a small dish; set aside.
2. Lay out the tortillas on a work surface. Spread the tortillas evenly with the butter, then sprinkle the cinnamon mixture on top.
3. Roll up the tortilla, then slice each into 8 pieces with a table knife. Place the pieces in a 9" pie pan and bake for about 8 minutes or until golden brown. Serve while still warm.

Nutritional information per serving:
Carbohydrates: 9 grams; Effective Carb Count: 2 grams;
Protein: 4 grams; Fat: 4 grams; Calories: 71

Easy Kefir Smoothie

Makes 8 servings

Kefir is a wonderful food! It is loaded with nutrition, and besides that, it tastes great. Enjoy this delicious drink as a snack or as a nutrient-packed part of breakfast.

8 cups kefir (1 quart)
¼ cup sugar-free specialty syrup (the kind used for flavored coffee)
1 teaspoon SteviaPlus

Combine all of the ingredients in a large pitcher. Chill and serve.

Nutritional information per serving:
Carbohydrates: 4 grams; Effective Carb Count: 4 grams;
Protein: 9 grams; Fat: 8 grams; Calories: 150

Reduced-Fat Variation:
Use low-fat kefir. Follow all remaining instructions as given.
Carbohydrates: 4 grams; Effective Carb Count: 4 grams;
Protein: 14 grams; Fat: 0 grams; Calories: 137

ELEPHANT EARS

Makes 4 servings

I remember going to the county fair when I was a child. The colorful Ferris wheel was enormous. The area where the food was prepared and eaten was full of both strange and familiar sights and smells. One of the strangest-sounding treats I experienced at the fair was also one of the yummiest—Elephant Ears!

> *Coconut oil or lard, for frying*
> *4 packets sucralose*
> *½ teaspoon SteviaPlus*
> *½ teaspoon ground cinnamon*
> *4 (6") low-carb tortillas*

1. In a large frying pan over medium heat, melt enough oil to cover the bottom about ½" deep.
2. Combine the sweeteners with the cinnamon in a small dish and set aside.
3. Place a tortilla in the oil and cook it on one side until it is golden, flip it, and cook it until it is golden on the second side, about 2 minutes total.
4. Remove the cooked tortilla to a plate lined with paper towels. Sprinkle each side with the cinnamon mixture.
5. Repeat with the remaining tortillas. Serve hot.

Nutritional information per serving:
Carbohydrates: 12 grams; Effective Carb Count: 3 grams;
Protein: 5 grams; Fat: 9 grams; Calories: 119

FAKE FUDGE

Makes 1 serving

Have you ever had one of those days when you just need something sweet? You really don't care what it is, but another meal without dessert is just not what you want? That was how this recipe came about. My kids beg for it! I can quadruple this recipe, and they will still be licking the bowl at the end. Hope you enjoy it, too!

2 tablespoons cream cheese
½ tablespoon cream
1 packet sucralose
¼ teaspoon SteviaPlus
½ tablespoon cocoa powder

Place the cream cheese in a small microwave-safe dish and warm for about 20 seconds in the microwave. Add the remaining ingredients and mix well.

Nutritional information per serving:
Carbohydrates: 2 grams; Effective Carb Count: 1 gram;
Protein: 3 grams; Fat: 12 grams; Calories: 126

Reduced-Fat Variation:
Use canned skim milk and reduced-fat cream cheese.
Follow all other instructions as given.
Carbohydrates: 3 grams; Effective Carb Count: 2 grams;
Protein: 3 grams; Fat: 4 grams; Calories: 49

GARLIC CHEESE DIP

Makes 12 servings

I am so fortunate to have wonderful folks who test recipes for me. One of my most faithful testers is Lori Rainey. Thank you, Lori, for sharing this yummy recipe! Serve this delicious dip with fresh veggies or pork rinds. For some yummy variations, you can add 1 tablespoon Golden Onions and Mushrooms (page 82), or ⅓ cup chopped, cooked bacon, or 2 tablespoons chopped green olives—or all of the above. You can also serve this as a hot dip by warming it in the oven or in a small slow cooker.

1 (8-ounce) package cream cheese, softened
½ cup sour cream
¼ teaspoon onion powder
¾ teaspoon garlic powder
4 drops (about ¹⁄₁₆ teaspoon) hot chili oil or a few grains of cayenne
1½ cups shredded cheese (a Colby–jack blend is best)

Stir the first 5 ingredients together in a medium-sized bowl. Add the shredded cheese and mix it well.

Nutritional information per serving:
Carbohydrates: 1 gram; Effective Carb Count: 1 gram;
Protein: 5 grams; Fat: 13 grams; Calories: 145

Reduced-Fat Variation:
Use reduced-fat versions of the cream cheese, sour cream, and cheese.
Follow all other instructions as given.
Carbohydrates: 1 gram; Effective Carb Count: 1 gram;
Protein: 6 grams; Fat: 6 grams; Calories: 78

HAYSTACKS

Makes 30 candies

Chocolate + coconut = Yum! For a really special treat, form the chocolate mixture around a whole almond before chilling. Keep these treats in the freezer; otherwise it is really easy to overindulge!

4 squares baking chocolate, unsweetened (I prefer Hershey's)
2 tablespoons unsalted butter
¼ cup coconut oil
2½ teaspoons SteviaPlus
16 packets sucralose
1/16 teaspoon sea salt
½ teaspoon vanilla extract
2 tablespoons milk and egg protein powder
¼ cup soy protein isolate
1¾ cups unsweetened coconut

1. Combine the chocolate, butter, and coconut oil in a microwave-safe bowl; microwave on high power for about 2½ minutes or until the chocolate melts, stirring partway through.
2. Add all the remaining ingredients *except* the coconut, and stir until they are smooth.
3. Add the coconut gradually, stirring the candy after each addition. After it is all incorporated, drop the candies by teaspoonfuls onto waxed paper and chill them in the refrigerator before serving.

Nutritional information per serving (1 piece of candy):
Carbohydrates: 2 grams; Effective Carb Count: 1 gram;
Protein: 2 grams; Fat: 8 grams; Calories: 78

LOW-CARB TORTILLA CHIPS

Makes about 10 servings

Pack these along with you as part of Taco Salad Tilikum (page 73), or you can enjoy them as an easy snack with salsa and sour cream or one of the dips from this book. This is a much more economical way to get them than buying the commercial low-carb tortilla chips that retail at nearly $4 a bag! Fresh always tastes better anyway.

10 (6") low-carb tortillas
Coconut oil or lard, for frying
Salt or seasoning salt, to taste

1. Using sharp kitchen scissors, cut the tortillas into wedges, about 8 per tortilla.
2. In a large frying pan over medium-low heat, melt enough oil to fill the pan about ¾" deep. Cook the tortilla chips until they are golden, about 30 seconds to 1 minute on each side, turning once during cooking. Drain on paper towels. Season as desired.
3. To store: Place the cooled chips in plastic storage bags, being careful that they are well sealed. They will stay fresh for about 3 days.

Nutritional information per serving:
Carbohydrates: 12 grams; Effective Carb Count: 3 grams;
Protein: 5 grams; Fat: 7 grams; Calories: 107

Reduced-Fat Variation:
Lay the cut tortilla pieces out on a baking sheet and spray each side with cooking oil spray. Bake them for about 5 to 7 minutes at 375°F, or until they are crisp and becoming golden.
Carbohydrates: 12 grams; Effective Carb Count: 3 grams;
Protein: 5 grams; Fat: 2 grams; Calories: 60

No-Bake Cookies, Low-Carbed

Makes about 34 cookies

This recipe came about as a request from Annette Wehland, a member of the *LowCarbEating.com* cooking forum. It is quick, easy, and yummy! A real winner.

½ tablespoon SteviaPlus
24 packets sucralose
⅓ cup cocoa powder
½ cup yogurt or kefir (coconut milk or cream would also work)
½ cup butter
½ cup creamy peanut butter
¾ cup unsweetened coconut
½ cup flaxseeds
¼ cup milk and egg protein powder
1 cup coarsely chopped almonds

1. Combine the SteviaPlus, sucralose, cocoa powder, yogurt, and butter in a medium-sized saucepan. Bring the mixture to a boil, stirring constantly. Allow it to boil for about 1 minute.
2. Remove the cocoa mixture from the heat and add the remaining ingredients, stirring well.
3. Drop the dough by teaspoonfuls onto waxed paper and allow the cookies to cool for approximately 1 hour at room temperature.
4. Package the cookies in serving-size portions and freeze in freezer bags for up to 1 month.

Nutrition Information per serving (1 cookie):
Carbohydrates: 3 grams; Effective Carb Count: 1 gram;
Protein: 3 grams; Fat: 9 grams; Calories: 98

NUTTY CARAMEL ROLL-UPS

Makes 4 servings

This is a fun quickie treat that will have everyone licking their fingers and smacking their lips. Just don't tell them it is low-carb!

1 recipe Caramel Nut Sauce (page 218)
2 (6") low-carb tortillas
½ teaspoon butter, plus extra for greasing
¼ teaspoon ground cinnamon
¼ teaspoon SteviaPlus
1 packet sucralose

1. Prepare the Caramel Nut Sauce (page 218) and set it aside. Butter a 9" pie plate and set it aside.
2. Lay 2 tortillas on a work surface. Divide the sauce evenly over half of each of the tortillas. Roll the up, starting with the saucy side. The sauce will spread out as you roll up the tortillas. Place the rolled tortillas into the buttered pie pan, seam-side down.
3. Spread the butter evenly over the tops of the rolls. Combine the cinnamon and sweeteners, and sprinkle them over the tops of the roll-ups.
4. Bake them in a 350°F oven for about 8 minutes, or until they are warmed through. Cut the roll-ups in half and serve.

Nutritional information per serving:
Carbohydrates: 6 grams; Effective Carb Count: 1 gram;
Protein: 3 grams; Fat: 2 grams; Calories: 36

ORANGE ESSENCE ALMONDS

Makes about 16 servings

I was chatting with some friends when I got the inspiration for this delicious treat. It makes a great portable snack and is terrific to bring to get-togethers as well. It is always a big hit!

1½ tablespoons coconut oil or butter
2 teaspoons orange extract (lemon works well, too)
1 pound (approximately 4 cups) raw almonds
8 packets sucralose
2 teaspoons SteviaPlus
¼ teaspoon ground cloves
Olive oil cooking spray (or coconut oil)

1. Preheat the oven to 350°F. Place the coconut oil into a microwave-safe bowl large enough to hold all the ingredients. Microwave the coconut oil on high power for about 1 minute or until it is melted.
2. Stir the extract into the melted oil. Add the nuts and stir well. Add the remaining seasonings, and mix well.
3. Pour the coated nuts onto a baking sheet that has been sprayed with cooking oil spray (or rubbed lightly with coconut oil), scraping the bowl well and spreading the nuts evenly over the sheet.
4. Bake the nuts for about 15 minutes, stirring once while cooking. Pour them at once into a heat-safe container, scraping any of the caramelized bits off the pan and into the bowl. Allow them to cool completely for best flavor and crunch.

Nutritional information per serving:
Carbohydrates: 6 grams; Effective Carb Count: 3 grams;
Protein: 6 grams; Fat: 16 grams; Calories: 179

RANCH ALMONDS

Makes 12 servings

This is a great snack or salad topper if slivered or sliced almonds are used. Try a variety of salad dressing mixes with your nuts, just watch out for sugar in the mixes!

3 cups raw almonds
2 tablespoons olive oil
1 packet ranch-style salad dressing mix

1. Preheat oven to 350°F. Place the almonds and olive oil into a bowl. Stir well to coat the almonds evenly with the oil. Pour the salad dressing mix over the nuts and stir well to coat evenly.
2. Spread out the almonds on a baking sheet and bake them for about 7 to 10 minutes. Cool them completely before serving. Store in an airtight container for up to 2 weeks.

Nutritional information per serving:
Carbohydrates: 9 grams; Effective Carb Count: 5 grams;
Protein: 7 grams; Fat: 21 grams; Calories: 236

ROASTED PECANS

4 servings

This is a yummy snack and is an integral component of Pumpkin Granola (page 48). Be careful not to eat them until they are cooled or you'll burn your tongue. It will be difficult, but I *suppose* it can be done!

¼ cup coconut oil or butter
4 cups (about 1 pound) pecan pieces, broken up
1 teaspoon SteviaPlus
8 packets sucralose
1 teaspoon ground cinnamon
1 teaspoon vanilla extract

1. Preheat oven to 325°F. Soften the coconut oil in the microwave for about 30 seconds, if necessary. Place the pecans into a mixing bowl. Pour the oil over the pecans and stir well to coat them evenly. Add the remaining ingredients, stirring them well to coat evenly.
2. Spread out the coated nuts on a baking sheet and bake them for 10 minutes. Cool them thoroughly before eating.
3. To store them for later use, package the nuts into sandwich-sized plastic bags. Place them into the freezer until you are ready to use them.

Nutritional information per serving:
Carbohydrates: 5 grams; Effective Carb Count: 3 grams;
Protein: 2 grams; Fat: 21 grams; Calories: 207

SAVORY PECANS

Makes 8 servings

For an extra kick, add ¼ teaspoon each of garlic powder and red pepper flakes. You may also grind your spices in a blender or spice grinder. They'll stick better to the nuts.

2 cups pecan halves (walnuts would also work)
½ tablespoon dried rosemary
1 teaspoon dried thyme leaves
¾ teaspoon seasoning salt
1 tablespoon olive oil

1. Preheat oven to 350°F. Combine all of the ingredients in a large bowl or plastic bag and mix them well.
2. Bake them for about 10 minutes or until the kitchen is filled with wonderful smells and the nuts are golden.

Nutritional information per serving:
Carbohydrates: 5 grams; Effective Carb Count: 3 grams;
Protein: 2 grams; Fat: 20 grams; Calories: 196

SCRUMPTIOUS COCONUT DROPS

Makes about 24 candies

I was having a tough time thinking of a name for these candies. My eleven-year-old daughter, being silly, suggested, "Yummy, Sweet, Up and Downy, Roundy-Roundy, Melt-in-Your-Mouth, Coconut Candy." Call them what you want, just be sure to share! You can use other flavors of sugar-free syrup; I just particularly like the German chocolate. Freeze the extras, or you might be tempted to eat them all!

2 tablespoons coconut oil
⅔ cup German chocolate–flavored sugar-free
specialty syrup (the kind for coffee)
1 cup unsweetened shredded coconut
½ cup milk and egg protein powder
½ teaspoon SteviaPlus
½ teaspoon vanilla extract
Pinch salt (way less than ⅛ teaspoon)

1. Place the coconut oil into a microwave-safe container and microwave for about 45 seconds, or until it is melted. Stir in the syrup.
2. Add the remaining ingredients and stir well.
3. Drop the coconut mixture by rounded teaspoonfuls onto waxed paper. Chill in the refrigerator. They will be soft at room temperature, firm when chilled. You may freeze any extras in sealable plastic storage bags.

Nutritional information per serving:
Carbohydrates: 1 gram; Effective Carb Count: 0 grams;
Protein: 2 grams; Fat: 3 grams; Calories: 38

SHARRON'S BEEF JERKY

Makes about 36 servings

Make this and you'll have snacks for a couple of weeks. You can even use it for quick meals when you have absolutely no time to cook. A few pieces of beef jerky, some almonds, and some celery sticks, and you're good to go!

3½–4 pounds beef steak or roast (avoid a heavily marbled piece)
4 tablespoons fresh-squeezed lime juice
½ teaspoon garlic granules or 1 clove garlic, minced
1½ teaspoons lemon pepper
1 tablespoon seasoning salt
1 tablespoon dried minced onion or ¼ cup minced fresh onion
1 teaspoon ground ginger
½ teaspoon mustard powder
1 teaspoon hot chili oil or a pinch of cayenne
⅛–¼ teaspoon SteviaPlus or ½–2 packets sucralose (to taste)
1½ cups Rich Stock, beef (page 166) or commercially prepared beef broth

1. Make thin slices of beef by slicing it at an angle across the grain of the meat. Some prefer to partially freeze the meat before slicing, but I find that slicing at an angle with a very sharp knife does just fine. (It may also be possible to get the butcher to slice it for you for free when you buy it, but then you can't be so particular about getting the fat out.) Set the beef aside.
2. Place the remaining ingredients in a large nonmetal bowl with a lid, stirring well to combine. Add the beef, mixing thoroughly.
3. Allow the meat to marinate in the refrigerator at least overnight, turning and shaking the container occasionally to stir it. If the meat is very fresh, it can be marinated up to 3 days. The flavors will intensify the longer it remains in the marinade.
4. When you are ready to dry the meat, lay it out on the drying racks of a food dehydrator. Discard the marinade. Dry the meat for about 4 to 6 hours. Alternatively, it may be dried on baking sheets in an oven set on the lowest setting for about 4 hours.

5. To test the jerky for doneness: The meat should no longer be mushy. It should be firm, but not crisp. Turn off the dehydrator when you believe the meat is getting close to being done and allow it to cool. The meat will continue to firm up as it cools. The jerky should be bendable and show fibers when it is bent. (That is how you will know when it is done.) After this step, I usually have a few pieces that need a little more dehydration. I remove the pieces that are done drying and turn the machine back on for about 30 minutes with the remaining pieces still in it. Then I turn it off and allow it to cool back down again. That usually finishes the job. Store the jerky in a plastic bag in the refrigerator.

Nutritional information per serving:
Carbohydrates: 0 grams; Effective Carb Count: 0 grams;
Protein: 11 grams; Fat: 4 grams; Calories: 81

SIMPLY GUACAMOLE

Makes 4 small servings

Simply Guacamole is simply delicious! This can be a snack or served with any of the Mexican recipes in this book.

1 ripe avocado
¼ cup sour cream
¼ teaspoon fresh-squeezed lemon juice
¼ teaspoon seasoning salt

In a small bowl, mash the avocado. Add the remaining ingredients and mix well.

Nutritional information per serving:
Carbohydrates: 4 grams; Effective Carb Count: 3 grams;
Protein: 1 gram; Fat: 11 grams; Calories: 112

Reduced-Fat Variation:
Use low-fat sour cream and follow all remaining instructions as given.
Carbohydrates: 4 grams; Effective Carb Count: 3 grams;
Protein: 1 gram; Fat: 8 grams; Calories: 86

SMOKED SALMON DIP

Makes 12 servings

This is a delightful way to use Smoked Salmon, the Easy Way (page 171). It is also a real winner if you need to take a little something to a potluck or a meeting!

1 cup smoked salmon
2 cups sour cream
1 tablespoon dried minced onion
1½ teaspoons dill weed
½ teaspoon grated orange rind (zest)
¼ teaspoon seasoning salt

Combine all the ingredients in a small bowl and mix them thoroughly. Chill for at least 30 minutes before serving. Serve with veggies or pork rinds.

Nutritional information per serving:
Carbohydrates: 2 grams; Effective Carb Count: 2 grams;
Protein: 3 grams; Fat: 9 grams; Calories: 97

Reduced-Fat Variation:
Use low-fat sour cream and follow all remaining instructions as given.
Carbohydrates: 2 grams; Effective Carb Count: 2 grams;
Protein: 3 grams; Fat: 1 gram; Calories: 28

SPINACH DIP

Makes 12 servings

Q M

Serve this dip with your favorite sliced meats and veggies. Cucumber and jicama slices are particularly nice! This is an integral part of Party Wraps (page 153).

½ cup mayonnaise
¾ cup sour cream
½ cup jicama, finely chopped
½ cup spinach, finely chopped (about 8 large leaves)
1 teaspoon dried chives or ½ tablespoon chopped fresh chives
1 teaspoon dried parsley flakes or ½ tablespoon chopped fresh parsley
1½ teaspoons dried minced onion
¼ teaspoon lemon pepper
½ teaspoon seasoning salt

In a medium-sized bowl, combine all of the ingredients and mix thoroughly. Chill the dip for about 30 minutes before serving.

Nutritional information per serving:
Carbohydrates: 1 gram; Effective Carb Count: 1 gram;
Protein: 1 gram; Fat: 11 grams; Calories: 100

Reduced-Fat Variation:
Use reduced-fat sour cream and mayonnaise.
Follow all remaining instructions as given.
Carbohydrates: 3 grams; Effective Carb Count: 3 grams;
Protein: 0 grams; Fat: 2 grams; Calories: 31

Extreme Lo-Carb Meals on the Go

SWEET-AND-SPICY ALMONDS, TAKE TWO

Serves 6

This is a wonderful, tasty, and nutritious treat! A great snack for that drive home.

3 tablespoons butter or coconut oil
2 cups blanched almonds
1½ teaspoons ground cinnamon
¾ teaspoon SteviaPlus
6 packets sucralose
1½ teaspoons grated orange rind (zest)
1½ teaspoons almond extract

1. Preheat oven to 325°F. Place the butter in a microwave-safe dish and heat it in the microwave for about 15 seconds, until melted.
2. Place the almonds into a bowl and pour the butter over them, mixing well to coat the almonds evenly. Add the remaining ingredients and mix well.
3. Spread the almonds onto a baking sheet and bake them for about 10 minutes. Cool them thoroughly before serving.
4. To package them up for later use, divide up the nuts into sealable plastic bags and store in the freezer for up to a month.

Nutritional information per serving:
Carbohydrates: 5 grams; Effective Carb Count: 2 grams;
Protein: 5 grams; Fat: 15 grams; Calories: 167

TOASTED SOYBEANS AND NUTS

Makes about 8 servings

There is a lot of hullabaloo about soybeans. If you get online you can read vastly differing opinions—everything from soybeans are killers to they are the greatest boon to humankind! All are adamant about their views. When I was first exposed to this information, I asked my naturopathic physician at the time what his view was. He replied, "Yes, there is a lot of debate about soybeans. My thought is that a little bit occasionally isn't going to hurt. Don't eat it every day, and you will be fine." Works for me!

Olive oil cooking spray
1 cup Precooked Soybeans (page 161) or
about 1 (8-ounce) can soybeans, drained
1 tablespoon, plus 1 teaspoon olive oil
½ teaspoon seasoning salt
1 teaspoon Old Bay Seasoning
¼ teaspoon lemon pepper
¼ teaspoon garlic granules
½ cup raw pumpkin kernels
¼ cup raw sunflower kernels
¼ teaspoon sea salt
¼ teaspoon dried thyme

1. Preheat the oven to 400°F.
2. In a medium-sized mixing bowl, combine the beans, 1 table-spoon olive oil, seasoning salt, Old Bay Seasoning, lemon pepper, and garlic. Spread this mixture onto a baking sheet that has been sprayed with cooking oil spray. Bake them at 400°F for 20 minutes, stirring partway through. The beans should begin to brown and become *slightly* crisp.

>>

3. In the same mixing bowl, combine the pumpkin kernels, sunflower seeds, 1 teaspoon olive oil, salt, and thyme. Stir them well and add them to the beans on the baking sheet. Bake them for about 8 to 10 minutes or until they are golden brown. (Be very careful to not overcook them. They go from being perfectly golden to scorched very quickly!)
4. Pour the mix into a bowl and let it cool partially before serving.
5. These may be divided up into snack-sized plastic bags for quick and easy snacks.

Nutritional information per serving:
Carbohydrates: 4 grams; Effective Carb Count: 2 grams;
Protein: 6 grams; Fat: 10 grams; Calories: 120

ZINGY PUMPKIN KERNELS

Makes about 8 servings

You might be wondering about my using coconut oil in all sorts of "savory" dishes, rather than just the sweet ones. A common misconception is that coconut oil gives a sweet taste to everything. I don't use virgin coconut oil—the kind with the flavor and aroma of coconuts—for my savory cooking. Instead, I use expeller-pressed coconut oil. It doesn't have any taste or smell, and is neutral in foods.

1 teaspoon coconut oil or butter
8 drops hot chili oil (about ⅛ teaspoon) or about 1/16 teaspoon cayenne
2 cups raw pumpkin kernels
2 teaspoons Old Bay Seasoning
½ teaspoon seasoning salt
¼ teaspoon lemon pepper
⅛ teaspoon garlic granules

1. Preheat oven to 350°F. Put the coconut oil into a microwave-safe dish large enough to accommodate all the ingredients. Microwave the oil on high for about 45 seconds, or until it is melted.
2. Add the hot chili oil to the melted coconut oil and swirl the bowl to mix it. Add the pumpkin kernels and stir well. Add the remaining seasonings and mix well.
3. Pour the pumpkin seeds onto a baking sheet and bake for about 8 to 10 minutes. If they begin popping, they are done. (Don't overcook them, or you will end up with hollow shells instead of meaty kernels.) Alternatively, you may cook them in a heavy-bottomed frying pan until they reach the desired doneness.
4. Pour them at once into a container to cool. Cool completely for the best flavor and crunch. Store them in a covered container for up to 2 weeks.

Nutritional information per serving:
Carbohydrates: 6 grams; Effective Carb Count: 5 grams;
Protein: 8 grams; Fat: 16 grams; Calories: 193

ZUCCHINI NUT BREAD

Makes 12 servings

When I was away at college, my mother used to bake her special Zucchini Nut Bread and send it to me as a care package. All my friends always knew when I had received a package, and always begged for some of my mom's bread. Enjoy this delicious bread as a great quick snack straight from the freezer.

Dry ingredients:
1 cup ground almonds
½ cup soy protein isolate
1 teaspoon ground cinnamon
½ teaspoon baking soda
¼ teaspoon baking powder
½ teaspoon sea salt
½ teaspoon ground nutmeg
1 tablespoon SteviaPlus
2 teaspoons Sweet & Slender
½ cup pecans, broken up

Wet ingredients:
1 cup shredded, unpeeled zucchini
1 egg
¼ cup butter, melted
¼ teaspoon grated lemon or orange rind (zest)
Olive oil cooking spray or butter

1. Preheat oven to 350°F. Mix the dry ingredients in a large mixing bowl. In another bowl, combine the wet ingredients. Pour the wet ingredients into the dry and stir until just combined. Pour into an 8" x 4" x 2" loaf pan that has been sprayed with cooking oil or buttered lightly.
2. Bake it for about 40 to 50 minutes or until a toothpick inserted into the center comes out clean. Cool the bread by laying the loaf pan on its side on a wire rack until it can be touched with bare hands, then inverting the bread quickly onto the cooling rack. Using another rack, turn the bread so it is right-side up. Slice and serve with butter.
3. To freeze for individual servings, slice the loaf and wrap each slice in plastic wrap. Place the slices into a freezer bag. The bread may be kept in the freezer for up to 1 month.

Nutritional information per serving:
Carbohydrates: 4 grams; Effective Carb Count: 2 grams; Protein: 8 grams; Fat: 13 grams; Calories: 157

Reduced-Fat Variation:
Use unsweetened applesauce instead of melted butter.
Follow all other instructions as given.
Carbohydrates: 4 grams; Effective Carb Count: 2 grams; Protein: 8 grams; Fat: 9 grams; Calories: 125

We all have times that we have to entertain, and
other times when we really want some dessert.
Enjoy yourself without being a slave to the kitchen!

Simple Desserts

BASIC PIE CRUST

Makes one 9" to 10" pie crust, 8 servings

This recipe is tried and true! I use it as my base for everything that gets thrown into a shell! It is superduper easy if you have preground almonds available. It takes way less than 10 minutes to make. In fact, if you are a die-hard "make-ahead" person, you could even mix this up in multiple batches, omitting the butter, and refrigerate or freeze the mix until you are ready to use it.

1 cup ground almonds (not blanched)
½ cup soy protein isolate
1 teaspoon SteviaPlus
4 packets sucralose
½ teaspoon ground cinnamon
6 tablespoons butter, room temperature

1. For a pie that will not be baked after the filling is added to the crust (baked crust): Combine the crust ingredients with a pastry blender or food processor and press into a 9" to 10" pie pan. Bake for 5 minutes at 450°F. Cool the crust completely before adding the filling.
2. For a pie that will be baked after the filling is added (unbaked crust): Follow the instructions in step 1, but don't bake the shell. Fill and bake the pie as directed in the pie recipe you are following.

Nutritional information per serving:
Carbohydrates: 3 grams; Effective Carb Count: 1 gram;
Protein: 10 grams; Fat: 17 grams; Calories: 200

Busy Day Cake

Makes 9 servings

I think everyone must have a *Better Homes and Gardens* cookbook!
I received mine as a wedding gift nearly two decades ago. Thanks to
Better Homes and Gardens for the inspiration for this cake!

⅓ cup coconut oil or butter, plus extra for greasing
⅓ cup soy protein isolate, plus extra for flouring
2 tablespoons vital wheat gluten flour
1 cup ground almonds
2 teaspoons baking powder
¼ teaspoon sea salt
¾ teaspoon SteviaPlus
6 packets sucralose
½ cup cream thinned with water to make ¾ cup
2 eggs
1½ teaspoons vanilla extract

Optional toppings:
Sucralose
Sugar-free specialty syrup (the kind for coffee)
Cream

1. Preheat the oven to 375°F. Grease a 9" x 9" x 2" pan and sprinkle
   it with soy protein isolate.
2. In a medium-sized mixing bowl, combine all of the ingredients
   except the optional toppings. Mix on medium speed until they are
   combined. Continue mixing for 2 minutes more. Pour the batter
   into the prepared pan and bake it for about 25 to 30 minutes,
   until a toothpick inserted in the center comes out clean.
3. Serve it as is, or with a sprinkling of sucralose. You can also top
   individual pieces with a drizzle of specialty syrup and a drizzle
   of cream. Enjoy!

Nutritional information per serving:
Carbohydrates: 5 grams; Effective Carb Count: 4 grams;
Protein: 12 grams; Fat: 20 grams; Calories: 234

CARAMEL APPLE CHEESECAKE

Makes 8 servings

For our seventeenth wedding anniversary, my husband and I were treated to a special dinner cruise. It was amazing! We floated down the beautiful Willamette River and dined on fabulous fare. At the end of our meal, we shared a piece of Caramel Apple Cheesecake. It was most assuredly not a low-carb item. This one, though, most assuredly is. This is a fabulous dessert for special occasions.

1 recipe Basic Pie Crust (page 214), unbaked
1 apple, peeled, cored, and sliced (about 1½ cups)
2 (8-ounce) packages cream cheese, room temperature
1 cup sour cream, room temperature
½ teaspoon vanilla extract
8 packets sucralose
1 teaspoon SteviaPlus
2 tablespoons milk and egg protein powder
¼ teaspoon sea salt
2 eggs, room temperature
¼ cup heavy cream, room temperature
Caramel Nut Sauce (page 218)

1. Follow the crust instructions for an unbaked shell. Refrigerate the crust while preparing the filling.
2. Preheat oven to 375°F. Place the apple slices into a microwave-safe dish with a lid. Microwave them on high power for about 1½ minutes, until they are just beginning to soften.
3. In a large mixing bowl, with an electric mixer beat the cream cheese, sour cream, and vanilla on medium-low speed until fluffy, about 2 minutes. (It is terribly important to have the filling ingredients at room temperature. A cheesecake is simply a thing that cannot be rushed!)
4. In a small bowl, combine the sucralose, SteviaPlus, milk and egg protein, and salt. Gradually add these dry ingredients to the cream cheese mixture, beating only until combined.

5. Combine the eggs and the cream in another small bowl, and beat them well with a fork. Add the eggs and cream to the cream cheese mixture and beat on low speed until it is just combined.

6. Spread the apples evenly over the crust, then pour the filling over the apples. Bake it for about 20 minutes. The sides should be puffy and the center still slightly jiggly. Leave the cheesecake in the oven and turn the oven off, leaving the door slightly ajar, for about 20 minutes. Remove the cheesecake from the oven and cool it thoroughly on a wire rack, then chill it in the refrigerator for at least 4 hours.

7. Prepare the Caramel Nut Sauce (page 218) according to the directions. Drizzle the sauce over the slices of cheesecake as they are served.

Nutritional information per serving:
Carbohydrates: 10 grams; Effective Carb Count: 7 grams;
Protein: 9 grams; Fat: 50 grams; Calories: 549

CARAMEL NUT SAUCE

Makes enough to cover 1 cheesecake, 8 servings

This simple little sauce is terrific on Caramel Apple Cheesecake (page 216), but can also be used to top Vanilla Yogurt (page 234) or cottage cheese. My kids actually prefer to just eat it off the spoon! If you want it without nuts, follow the same instructions, though you may need to increase the xanthan gum. It may also be prepared in the microwave.

1 tablespoon butter
¼ cup chopped or sliced nuts (almonds, walnuts, or pecans)
Pinch sea salt (way less than ⅛ teaspoon)
4 tablespoons caramel-flavored sugar-free specialty syrup
⅛ teaspoon xanthan gum

1. Melt the butter in a small saucepan over medium-low heat. Add the nuts and salt, and cook them until they are becoming golden, about 3 minutes. Don't allow the butter to brown, and keep the temperature pretty low. Remove the pan from the heat for about 1 minute.
2. Pour the syrup into the pan. Place it back on the burner and allow it to simmer for a few seconds before gently sprinkling the xanthan gum over the sauce. Stir well and remove from the heat.
3. Cool it partially before serving.

Nutritional information per serving:
Carbohydrates: 1 gram; Effective Carb Count: 0 grams;
Protein: 1 gram; Fat: 4 grams; Calories: 40

COCONUT ALMOND DELIGHTS

Makes 24 candies

You can make these delicious treats for your sweetie on Valentine's Day or just as a treat for yourself. The really nice thing about these, besides the fact that they are yummy, is that they won't break the carb or calorie bank!

For the filling:
2 tablespoons coconut oil
⅔ cup German chocolate–flavored sugar-free specialty syrup
(the kind for coffee)
1 cup unsweetened shredded coconut
½ cup milk and egg protein powder
½ teaspoon SteviaPlus
½ teaspoon vanilla extract
Pinch salt (way less than ⅛ teaspoon)
24 almonds

For the chocolate coating:
2 squares baking chocolate, unsweetened (I prefer Hershey's)
1 tablespoon unsalted butter
1 teaspoon SteviaPlus
7 packets sucralose
A few grains sea salt (way less than a pinch)
⅛ teaspoon vanilla extract
½ tablespoon milk and egg protein powder

1. Place the coconut oil into a microwave-safe container and microwave it for about 45 seconds or until it is melted. Stir in the syrup.
2. Add all the remaining filling ingredients *except* the almonds and stir well.
3. Drop the coconut mixture by rounded teaspoonfuls onto waxed paper (or parchment paper). Press an almond onto the top of each coconut mound and round the candy into a little ball. Let the candies rest on the waxed paper while preparing the coating.

4. Combine the chocolate and butter in a microwave-safe bowl and microwave on high power for about 1½ minutes or until the chocolate melts, stirring partway through. Add the remaining coating ingredients and stir until they are smooth.

5. Drop the coconut balls into the chocolate. Using two forks, drizzle the coating over the top of the coconut ball then lift the candy out of the chocolate, holding it by the tips of the forks and allowing the excess chocolate to drip off. Place the candy onto a plate lined with waxed paper, and chill them for 2 hours before serving. You may freeze any extras in zippered plastic storage bags.

Nutritional information per serving:

Carbohydrates: 2 grams; Effective Carb Count: 1 gram;
Protein: 2 grams; Fat: 5 grams; Calories: 55

CREAMY THREE-FLAVORED PUDDING

Makes 4 servings

One day I wanted some dessert, and I happened to have a partial can of coconut milk. This was the result. I hope you enjoy this simple dessert as much as my children and I do!

1 cup coconut milk
¼ cup caramel-flavored sugar-free specialty syrup
(the kind used for coffee)
½ teaspoon SteviaPlus
¼ cup creamy peanut butter
Pinch sea salt (way less than ⅛ teaspoon)
2 egg yolks

1. Combine the coconut milk, syrup, SteviaPlus, peanut butter, and salt in a small saucepan. Bring it to a boil. Reduce the heat, but allow it to continue to boil for about 2 to 3 minutes, until it starts to thicken. Remove the pan from the heat.
2. Have the yolks ready in a small bowl (a measuring cup works well). Add about ¼ cup of the hot pudding mixture to the yolks, mixing well. Pour the pudding-yolks mixture into the hot pudding in the pan and stir well.
3. Pour the hot pudding into small bowls and chill them in the refrigerator for about 30 minutes until set.

Nutritional information per serving:
Carbohydrates: 7 grams; Effective Carb Count: 5 grams;
Protein: 7 grams; Fat: 25 grams; Calories: 234

GERMAN CHOCOLATE RASPBERRY YOGURT

Makes 8 servings

Let's face it—there are certain times when we really want some chocolate! It's best to avoid the sugar-free candies that are sweetened with maltitol and other sugar alcohols, because they can cause bad cravings. This delicious treat gives you a chocolate fix without the side effects. Also, a note about the carb values of yogurt, kefir, and buttermilk: Research has shown them to be valued at 4 grams per cup, so all of the recipes have been calculated at that level.

1 quart yogurt
2 tablespoons raspberry-flavored sugar-free specialty syrup
(the kind for coffee)
⅔ cup German chocolate–flavored sugar-free specialty syrup
(as above)

Dump the yogurt into a mixing bowl. Add the syrups and mix well. Eat. Enjoy!

Nutritional information per serving:
Carbohydrates: 2 grams; Effective Carb Count: 2 grams;
Protein: 4 grams; Fat: 4 grams; Calories: 75

Reduced-Fat Variation:
Use low-fat yogurt. Follow all other instructions as given.
Carbohydrates: 2 grams; Effective Carb Count: 2 grams;
Protein: 7 grams; Fat: 0 grams; Calories: 68

GREEN APPLE DELIGHT

Serves 4

This is a very easy dessert or snack that will make you feel like you are being totally decadent! For a special treat for the kids, serve this with apple chips, which are available in most produce departments. You may use ricotta cheese instead of cottage cheese, if you wish.

2 cups cottage cheese
¼ to ½ cup sugar-free green apple specialty syrup (the kind for coffee)
1 teaspoon ground cinnamon

Divide the cottage cheese equally between 4 serving dishes. Drizzle the syrup over the top, and sprinkle each with cinnamon.

Nutritional information per serving:
Carbohydrates: 5 grams; Effective Carb Count: 5 grams;
Protein: 16 grams; Fat: 2 grams; Calories: 103

Reduced-Fat Variation:
Use low-fat cottage cheese. Follow all other instructions as given.
Carbohydrates: 4 grams; Effective Carb Count: 4 grams;
Protein: 14 grams; Fat: 1 gram; Calories: 83

Low-Carb Key Lime Pie

Makes 8 servings

Now, we can enjoy this yummy treat with a low-carb flair. When I made this low-carb version, I took it to a church potluck. Several of my friends, who do not eat low-carb, came up to me and told me this was the best lime pie they had ever tasted! Made my day. As an alternative you can use fresh lemon juice and homemade kefir or yogurt cheese instead of the cream cheese for a terrific variation. Just remember, when you are going to serve this, keep your carb and calorie levels lower throughout the rest of the day.

1 recipe Basic Pie Crust (page 214), baked
2 (8-ounce) packages cream cheese, softened
1¼ teaspoons SteviaPlus
14 packets sucralose
½ cup coconut milk
½ cup fresh-squeezed lime juice
1 packet unflavored gelatin
½ cup boiling water
2 drops green food coloring (optional)
1 drop yellow food coloring (optional)

1. Prepare the crust according to the recipe directions for a baked shell.
2. Combine the cream cheese and sweeteners in a large mixing bowl. With an electric mixer, beat until fluffy, about 1 minute.
3. While continuing to mix, slowly pour in the coconut milk and lime juice, mixing until well incorporated.
4. Stir the gelatin into the water, then pour it into the filling mixture, mixing thoroughly. Add the food coloring, if desired.
5. Pour the filling into the pie crust and chill it in the refrigerator until set, about 1 hour. Allow the pie to rest at room temperature for about 5 minutes before slicing and serving.

Nutritional information per serving:
Carbohydrates: 7 grams; Effective Carb Count: 5 grams;
Protein: 5 grams; Fat: 40 grams; Calories: 439

MOCHA CHEESECAKE

Makes 12 servings

This is a truly decadent dessert that is simple to prepare. It is true, it cannot be rushed, but there is nothing difficult about it, except being patient! Prepare this the night before you have company and you will be sure to "wow" them with this decadent, albeit sugar-free, dessert.

1 recipe Basic Pie Crust (page 214), unbaked
3½ tablespoons cocoa powder
2 (8-ounce) packages cream cheese, room temperature
1 cup sour cream, room temperature
½ teaspoon vanilla extract
8 packets sucralose
1½ teaspoons SteviaPlus
2 tablespoons milk and egg protein powder
1 tablespoon instant coffee crystals
¼ teaspoon sea salt
2 eggs, plus 1 egg yolk, room temperature
¼ cup heavy cream, room temperature

1. Follow the crust instructions for an unbaked shell, adding 1 tablespoon cocoa powder during the mixing. Refrigerate the crust while preparing the filling.
2. In a large mixing bowl, beat the cream cheese, sour cream, and vanilla with an electric mixer on medium-low speed until fluffy, about 2 minutes. (It is terribly important to have the filling ingredients at room temperature. A cheesecake is simply a thing that cannot be rushed!)
3. In a small bowl, combine the remaining 2½ tablespoons cocoa, the sucralose, SteviaPlus, milk and egg protein, coffee crystals, and salt. Gradually add these dry ingredients to the cheese mixture, beating only until combined.
4. Combine the eggs and the cream in another small bowl and mix them well with a fork. Add the eggs and cream to the cheese mixture and beat on low speed until it is just combined.

5. Pour the filling into the chilled pie crust and bake it for about 20 minutes. The sides should be puffy and the center still slightly jiggly. Leave the cheesecake in the oven and turn the oven off, leaving the door slightly ajar, for about 20 minutes. Remove the cheesecake from the oven and cool it thoroughly on a wire rack, then chill in the refrigerator for at least 4 hours.

Nutritional information per serving:
Carbohydrates: 5 grams; Effective Carb Count: 3 grams;
Protein: 6 grams; Fat: 31 grams; Calories: 346

PECAN PIE

Makes 8 servings

A traditional Southern dessert, especially at the holidays, pecan pie is something that often causes folks to stray from their low-carb ways. Now they can have their pie, and eat it, too! If you don't have any caramel syrup on hand, you can use gingerbread—or toffee-flavored sugar-free syrup.

> 1 recipe Basic Pie Crust (page 214), unbaked
> ¼ teaspoon xanthan gum
> 1 cup cottage cheese
> 1 teaspoon SteviaPlus
> 1 tablespoon milk and egg protein powder
> 1 teaspoon vanilla extract
> 3 eggs
> 2 tablespoons butter, melted
> 1 cup caramel-flavored sugar-free specialty syrup (the kind for coffee)
> 1¼ cups pecan halves (walnuts work well, too)

1. Prepare the pie crust as an unbaked shell, adding the xanthan gum to the dry ingredients before adding the butter. Set the shell aside.
2. In a mixing bowl, combine the cottage cheese, SteviaPlus, milk and egg protein, and vanilla with an electric mixer on medium-low speed. Add the eggs and beat until combined, about 45 seconds.
3. Pour in the melted butter, and mix briefly. Add the syrup and mix on low speed until it is well combined, scraping the bowl often.
4. Stir in the pecans by hand. Pour the filling into the crust, making sure the pecans are evenly dispersed across the top of the pie. Bake it at 375°F for 40 to 45 minutes, or until a toothpick inserted in the center of the pie, comes out clean.

Nutritional information per serving:
Carbohydrates: 8 grams; Effective Carb Count: 5 grams;
Protein: 8 grams; Fat: 33 grams; Calories: 392

QUICK AND EASY RED PIE

Makes 8 servings

Well, it doesn't have to be red! It could be red, green, blue, purple, or whatever color of gelatin dessert you choose. I often make this pie when I find out at the last minute that I need to take a dessert somewhere. It is always a big hit!

For the crust:
¾ cup ground almonds
⅓ cup soy protein isolate
¾ teaspoon SteviaPlus
3 packets sucralose
¼ cup butter

For the filling:
1 (8-ounce) package cream cheese, softened
¼ cup sour cream
½ teaspoon SteviaPlus or 2 packets sucralose
1 (0.3- to 0.44-ounce) packet sugar-free gelatin dessert (4-serving size)
½ cup boiling water

1. Combine the crust ingredients in a food processor, or by hand, and mix until they are well blended. Press the crust into a small pie pan, approximately 7 inches across. Bake the crust at 400°F for about 8 minutes or until it starts to brown. Remove it from the oven and place it on a cooling rack.
2. Meanwhile, in a small mixing bowl, combine the cream cheese, sour cream, and SteviaPlus with an electric mixer on medium speed until smooth. Dissolve the gelatin in the water. Add it very slowly to the cream cheese mixture, mixing on low speed until well combined. Immediately pour the filling into the pie crust. (The crust does not need to be cooled before pouring the gelatin mixture into it.)

3. Depending upon how soon you need the dessert, you may either put it into the freezer for about 30 minutes or refrigerate it for about an hour or so, until it is set and chilled. Remove the pie from the refrigerator or freezer about 5 minutes before serving, so that it is easier to dish up.

Nutritional information per serving:
Carbohydrates: 4 grams; Effective Carb Count: 3 grams;
Protein: 10 grams; Fat: 24 grams; Calories: 258

Reduced-Fat Variation:
Use reduced-fat cream cheese and low-fat sour cream.
Follow all other instructions as given.
Carbohydrates: 4 grams; Effective Carb Count: 3 grams;
Protein: 11 grams; Fat: 19 grams; Calories: 220

SIMPLY CHEESECAKE

Makes 12 servings

M

Extreme Lo-Carb Meals on the Go

You may be wondering why I don't offer reduced-fat variations for many of my more decadent desserts. The reason is exactly that— they are decadent! They need to be saved for special occasions.

1 recipe Basic Pie Crust (page 214), unbaked
2 (8-ounce) packages cream cheese, room temperature
1 cup sour cream, room temperature
½ teaspoon vanilla extract
8 packets sucralose
1 teaspoon SteviaPlus
2 tablespoons milk and egg protein powder
¼ teaspoon sea salt
2 eggs, plus 1 egg yolk, room temperature
¼ cup heavy cream, room temperature

1. Follow the crust instructions for an unbaked shell. Refrigerate the crust while preparing the filling.
2. In a large mixing bowl, beat the cream cheese, sour cream, and vanilla with an electric mixer on medium-low speed until fluffy, about 2 minutes.
3. In a small bowl, combine the sucralose, SteviaPlus, milk and egg protein, and salt. Gradually add these dry ingredients to the cream cheese mixture, beating only until combined.
4. Combine the eggs and the cream in another small bowl and mix them well with a fork. Add the eggs and cream to the cream cheese mixture and beat on low speed until it is just combined.
5. Pour the filling into the chilled pie crust and bake it at 375°F for about 20 minutes. The sides should be puffy and the center still slightly jiggly. Leave the cheesecake in the oven and turn the oven off, leaving the door slightly ajar, for about 20 minutes. Remove the cheesecake from the oven and cool it thoroughly on a wire rack, then chill it in the refrigerator for at least 4 hours.

Nutritional information per serving:
Carbohydrates: 4 grams; Effective Carb Count: 3 grams;
Protein: 6 grams; Fat: 31 grams; Calories: 341

SIMPLY DELICIOUS YOGURT PARFAITS

Makes 4 servings

My children were asking for dessert one evening and my friend mentioned how she loves those prepared yogurt parfaits that are available at fast-food restaurants. I had just made a big batch of Pumpkin Granola (page 48) that day, and Vanilla Yogurt (page 234) the day before. I said, "I can do that!" So can you! This makes a great quick and easy snack or dessert.

4 cups Vanilla Yogurt (page 234)
1 cup blueberries or blackberries
1 cup Pumpkin Granola (page 48)

1. Divide the yogurt evenly between 4 dessert dishes.
2. Arrange the berries attractively around the edges of the parfaits.
3. Sprinkle the granola over the top and serve immediately.

Nutritional information per serving:
Carbohydrates: 14 grams; Effective Carb Count: 10 grams;
Protein: 13 grams; Fat: 19 grams; Calories: 290

Reduced-Fat Variation:
Use reduced-fat yogurt. Follow all remaining instructions as given.
Carbohydrates: 14 grams; Effective Carb Count: 11 grams;
Protein: 18 grams; Fat: 11 grams; Calories: 277

SNICKERS PIE

Makes 12 servings

I just love it when folks take my recipes and turn them into something new and wonderful! This is one such recipe. For a fantastic treat, freeze the pie before putting on the topping. Just be sure not to freeze a glass pan!

1 recipe Basic Pie Crust (page 214), baked
1 recipe Caramel Nut Sauce (page 218), using peanuts
instead of the nuts specified

For the filling:
½ cup creamy peanut butter
¾ cup butter, at room temperature
1 teaspoon SteviaPlus
8 packets sucralose
3 tablespoons unsweetened cocoa powder
1½ teaspoons vanilla extract
3 eggs

For the topping:
1 cup whipping cream
¼ teaspoon SteviaPlus or 1½ packets sucralose
2 tablespoons chopped peanuts

>>

1. Prepare the crust for a baked pie shell. Prepare the sauce as directed. Pour the Caramel Nut Sauce (page 218) into the baked pie crust and set aside.
2. In a large mixing bowl, cream the peanut butter, butter, SteviaPlus, and sucralose with an electric mixer on medium speed for about 1 minute. Add the cocoa powder and vanilla, mixing until combined. Add the eggs one at a time, beating for 5 minutes after each egg is added. Total mixing time for the filling will be 16 minutes. Pour the filling into the pie shell. Chill the pie in the refrigerator for at least 4 hours to set.
3. To prepare the topping, whip the cream in a small mixing bowl with an electric mixer until soft peaks form. Add the SteviaPlus and whip until combined. Spread the cream onto the chilled pie. Sprinkle the top of the pie with the chopped peanuts. Enjoy!

Nutritional information per serving:
Carbohydrates: 6 grams; Effective Carb Count: 3 grams;
Protein: 4 grams; Fat: 34 grams; Calories: 362

VANILLA YOGURT

Makes 4 servings

Besides being one of my favorite snacks, this makes a great sauce for pancakes, waffles, French toast, and the like (low-carb, of course!). It makes a nice dessert or addition to breakfast. You can also pour it over fruit for a fruit salad.

1 pint (2 cups) whole-milk yogurt
2½ teaspoons vanilla extract
¾ teaspoon Sweet & Slender
½ teaspoon SteviaPlus
Ground cinnamon, for garnish (optional)

In a small bowl, combine the yogurt, vanilla, Sweet & Slender, and SteviaPlus; mix well. Garnish the yogurt with cinnamon, if desired.

Nutritional information per serving:
Carbohydrates: 3 grams; Effective Carb Count: 2 grams;
Protein: 4 grams; Fat: 4 grams; Calories: 86

Reduced-Fat Variation:
Use nonfat yogurt and proceed as directed.
Carbohydrates: 3 grams; Effective Carb Count: 2 grams;
Protein: 7 grams; Fat: 0 grams; Calories: 79

YOGURT SWIRL DESSERT

Makes 4 servings

This is a quick dessert that gives a nice presentation. Think about color when choosing your syrup flavor; a darker or brighter color will be more striking against the yogurt. I'm particularly fond of huckleberry! If you have a real sweet tooth, you may wish to use more of the sugar-free syrup, up to ½ cup total.

1 quart plain yogurt
¼ cup sugar-free specialty syrup (the kind used in coffee)
1 cup Pumpkin Granola (page 48)

1. Divide the yogurt evenly between the dishes it will be served in.
2. Drizzle the syrup over the yogurt in the bowls. Using the end of a knife, swirl the syrup through the yogurt, so that it is evenly distributed but still in an attractive pattern.
3. Sprinkle the yogurt with the granola and serve immediately.

Nutritional information per serving:
Carbohydrates: 9 grams; Effective Carb Count: 7 grams;
Protein: 13 grams; Fat: 19 grams; Calories: 270

Reduced-Fat Variation:
Use reduced-fat yogurt. Follow all other instructions as given.
Carbohydrates: 9 grams; Effective Carb Count: 7 grams;
Protein: 18 grams; Fat: 11 grams; Calories: 157

Suggested Shopping List

Everyone has to go shopping!

Although this list is not comprehensive, I have done my best to list the items used in this book.

Sweeteners:

SteviaPlus (preferably the 4-ounce shaker bottle, but the
    packets may be substituted)
Sweet & Slender (as above)
Sucralose packets

Meats:

Eggs (organic, free-range if possible)
Beef
Chicken
Pork
Fish
Shrimp
Bacon and sausages (nitrate-free if possible)
Etc. . . . (use the best-quality fresh meat available)

Oils and fats:

Lard
Butter
Coconut oil (expeller-pressed is used for most recipes)
Olive oil
Mayonnaise
Olive oil cooking spray
Coconut milk

Dairy products:

Cream, heavy whipping
Half-and-half
Yogurt
Kefir and/or buttermilk
Cream cheese
Sour cream
Cottage cheese or Ricotta cheese
Cheeses—Parmesan, Colby, Monterey jack, etc.

Ethnic cookery items and more:

Bragg Liquid Aminos or soy sauce
Sesame oil
Hot chili oil or cayenne pepper
Sesame seeds
Tomato sauce (without sugar)
Canned tomatoes (without sugar)
Chipotle pepper granules
Chili powder, chilies, or jalapeño peppers
Cumin (ground)
Italian seasoning herb blend
Sauerkraut
Soybeans or small red beans (dried)
Low-carb tortillas
Low-carb pasta

Fruits and vegetables:

Salad greens (romaine or a good blend that is not heavy
on iceberg lettuce)
Lemons
Limes
Cabbage
Spinach (prewashed bagged is nice!)
Celery
Cauliflower
Broccoli
Zucchini (summer squash)
Cucumber
Radishes
Green beans (canned, frozen, or fresh)
Olives (canned, black)
Garlic
Onions
Avocados
Mushrooms
Canned pumpkin
Berries (blueberries, strawberries, blackberries,
cranberries, etc.)

Nuts

Raw almonds
Ground raw almonds
Sunflower seeds (hulled, raw or roasted)
Pumpkin seeds (hulled, raw)
Pecans

Herbs, seasonings, and miscellany:

Seasoning salt (without sugar or MSG)

Lemon pepper (without sugar or MSG)

Old Bay Seasoning

Garlic granules/powder

Mustard powder

Ground ginger

Dried onions

Dried parsley

Chives, rosemary, thyme (and other fresh herbs as available)

Cinnamon

Vanilla (real vanilla extract, not imitation!)

Arrowroot powder

Xanthan gum (or guar gum or one of the blends)

Soy protein isolate (in the beverage or nutrition section at most health food stores)

Milk and egg protein powder (one product—in the beverage or nutrition section at most health food stores)

Pork rinds

Sugar-free specialty syrups (Torani or Da Vinci preferred)

Unsweetened baking chocolate (Hershey's preferred)

Low-carb bread

Flaxseeds

Ranch salad dressing packets

Sample Menus

Everyone needs ideas now and again.

Daily Menus

Please note that I am not including desserts and snacks on these daily menus. Whether or not you have desserts and snacks is dependent upon your individual carb allowance and personal choice.

As a rule of thumb, I don't recommend eating dessert more often than once or twice a week at most. If you are planning a decadent dessert like Caramel Apple Cheesecake (page 216), then be sure and go lighter for the rest of the day in carbs, calories, and fat.

Snacks may or may not be necessary depending upon how long you go between meals. If lunch is at noon and dinner isn't until 8:00 P.M., then you will definitely need a snack! Most sources agree not to go any longer than six hours maximum, four hours ideally, without eating during waking hours. Some good snacks are listed in the "Snacks and Treats" section of this book. Always keep in mind your total carb allowance and what you are planning for the next meal when choosing your snacks.

■ ■ ■

Breakfast: Bacon and Three-Cheese Mini-Pizzas
(page 26)
Lunch: Creamy Coconut Chicken Salad
(page 64)
Dinner: Ranch Chops
(page 164)
Baked Winter Squash
(page 76)

■ ■ ■

Breakfast: Clubhouse Omelette
(page 37)
Lunch: Chicken Salad Sandwich Pizza Thingies
(page 125)
Small lettuce salad with Bacon Ranch Salad Dressing
(page 60)
Dinner: Beef and Broccoli in a Snap!
(page 110)

■ ■ ■

Breakfast: Flax Cereal
(page 42)
Hard cooked egg
Lunch: Chicken Club Salad
(page 61)
Dinner: Taco Casserole
(page 174)
Mexican Rice-Aflower
(page 88)

• • •

Breakfast: Quick and Easy Sausage Gravy
(page 51)
Cauliflower Hash Browns
(page 79)
Lunch: Egg Salad
(page 65)
Veggies, Now and Later
(page 100)
Spinach Dip
(page 206)
Dinner: Ranch Chicken
(page 163)
Easy-Peasy Greeny Beanies
(page 81)

• • •

Breakfast: Breakfast Burritos with Chorizo and Eggs
(page 32)
Lunch: Pizza Salad
(page 67)
Dinner: Great Grandma's German Sausage Bake
(page 139)

•••

Breakfast: Basic Scrambled Eggs
(page 28)
Lunch: Chicken Salad Sandwich Pizza Thingies
(page 125)
Sweet and Tangy Spinach Salad
(page 72)
Dinner: Adobo (Pork with Gravy)
(page 104)
Rice-Aflower
(page 92)

•••

Breakfast: Low-Carb Quesadillas
(page 46)
Lunch: Chicken Club Salad
(page 61)
Bacon Ranch Salad Dressing
(page 60)
Dinner: Easy Pot Roast and Veggies
(page 133)

■ ■ ■

Breakfast: Hearty Bacon and Eggs
(page 44)
Lunch: Piggies in Blankets
(page 156)
Veggies, Now and Later
(page 100)
Clubhouse Sauce
(page 63)
Dinner: Wonton Soup Without the Wontons
(page 183)

■ ■ ■

Breakfast: Pumpkin Granola
(page 48)
Simply Guacamole
(page 204)
Lunch: Taco Salad Tilikum
(page 73)
Dinner: Coney Dogs
(page 126)
Side salad with Bacon Ranch Salad Dressing
(page 60)

Conversion Charts for Sugar Substitutes
Used in This Book

We all need to be sweet once in a while!

Sucralose

I use the Splenda No Calorie Sweetener brand of sucralose product. Each packet weighs 1 gram. Please note, the pourable Splenda converts the same as regular sugar. It contains much more filler, thus more carbs, so I don't prefer it.

Stevia

I use the brand SteviaPlus by Wisdom Herbs (*www.wisdom herbs.com*). It is a stevia extract that is a fine white powder combined with a healthy dietary fiber called FOS. It is my understanding that FOS helps stabilize blood sugar levels. The FOS also makes this product milder and easier to cook with than other stevia products. Note: Other brands of stevia may not have the same conversion values.

Sweet & Slender

Sweet & Slender is a great new product on the market. It is made by the same manufacturer as SteviaPlus, Wisdom Herbs. It is made from an intensely sweet fruit, called *luo han guo*. While it is a terrific standalone sweetener or in combination with SteviaPlus, I prefer its use as a flavor enhancer. It just seems to bring out the best in foods!

Sucralose Conversion Chart

1 packet	=	2 teaspoons sugar
3 packets	=	2 tablespoons sugar
6 packets	=	¼ cup sugar
8 packets	=	⅓ cup sugar
12 packets	=	½ cup sugar
24 packets	=	1 cup sugar

SteviaPlus Conversion Chart for Use with Sucralose

⅛ teaspoon stevia	=	1 tablespoon plus ½ teaspoon sugar
¼ teaspoon stevia	=	2½ tablespoons sugar
½ teaspoon stevia	=	⅓ cup sugar
¾ teaspoon stevia	=	½ cup sugar
1 teaspoon stevia	=	⅔ cup sugar
½ tablespoon stevia	=	1 cup sugar
1 tablespoon stevia	=	2 cups sugar

Sweet & Slender Conversion Chart

⅛ teaspoon Sweet & Slender	=	1½ teaspoons sugar
¼ teaspoon Sweet & Slender	=	1 tablespoon sugar
½ teaspoon Sweet & Slender	=	2 tablespoons sugar
1 teaspoon Sweet & Slender	=	¼ cup sugar
½ tablespoon Sweet & Slender	=	⅓ cup sugar
2 teaspoons Sweet & Slender	=	½ cup sugar
1 tablespoon Sweet & Slender	=	⅔ cup sugar
1½ tablespoons Sweet & Slender	=	1 cup sugar

SteviaPlus Conversion Chart

¼ teaspoon SteviaPlus	=	2 teaspoons sugar
½ teaspoon SteviaPlus	=	1 tablespoon plus 1 teaspoon sugar
1 teaspoon SteviaPlus	=	2⅔ tablespoons sugar
1½ teaspoons SteviaPlus	=	¼ cup sugar
1 tablespoon SteviaPlus	=	½ cup sugar
1½ tablespoons SteviaPlus	=	¾ cup sugar
2 tablespoons SteviaPlus	=	1 cup sugar

Glossary of Unusual Items

Admittedly, there are some unusual items used in low-carb cooking. They are described here.

Soy Products

Because there is so much confusion about the different types of soy products that are available and their uses, I have included them here as a separate category. Not all of these soy products are used in this book. Many are simply provided for clarification of terms. The items used in this book are marked with an asterisk (*).

*Bragg Liquid Aminos:

A product available in health food stores and some major markets that has a similar flavor to soy sauce, but is not fermented.

soy flour:

A product derived from roasted soybeans. It comes in three forms: 1. Full fat or natural, containing all of the natural oils in the soybean, 2. Defatted, a product that has had the fat removed, 3. Lecithinated, a product which has had lecithin added to it.

soy protein concentrate:

A product containing 70 percent protein and retaining most of the soybean's natural fiber.

*soy protein isolate:

Protein that has been removed from defatted soy flakes. It contains 92 percent protein in the form of easily digested amino acids. The brand I use is labeled Soy Protein Powder and contains soy protein isolates, natural flavors, soy lecithin, bromelain, and papain. It has zero carbs per ½ cup and can be found in the health and fitness beverage aisle of most better stores. It can be substituted 1:1 for wheat flour, but since it doesn't have gluten, it will not rise like wheat flour does.

soy sauce:
A fermented salty tasting liquid.

tofu:
There are three types of tofu: 1. Firm tofu, which can be cubed or sliced and used in soups, stew, etc.; 2. Soft tofu, which is a blend of firm tofu and silken tofu; and 3. Silken tofu, which is a very soft product, similar in texture to sour cream.

*whole soybeans:
Raw, hard, dried legumes, available for purchase by the pound. Usually they are yellow, but can be brown or black as well.

Other Products Used in this Book

almonds, ground:
In the past, I have ground my own whole raw almonds because of the expense of purchasing the preground type. New products are available on the market and the prices are coming down. If you can afford it, preground almonds are a wonderful product that contains all the wonderful healthful fats and fiber of the almonds in their natural state, without the work of grinding them! Ground almonds are different from almond flour, which has the fat removed from it. Also, when a recipes says "ground almonds," what is meant is the amount of ground almonds that will fit in the measure, not the whole almonds measured, then ground.

arrowroot powder:

This is a thickener that has fewer carbs than white flour, but is not extremely low in carbs. However, it is the only choice for many who are allergic to wheat and xanthan gum. It contains 7 grams of carbs per tablespoon, but does require about ⅓ the amount to thicken as flour does. It is available at most natural food stores and is sold with the spices. Try to find it in the bulk aisles, however, as the bottled kind is extremely expensive.

bacon cured without nitrates:

It will be necessary to visit a natural foods store to purchase "uncured" bacon, but it is well worth the effort, as nitrates are known carcinogens.

coconut milk:

I use Chaokoh variety that I purchase from an Asian market. I like this particular one because of its thick, creamy texture. Other brands are available at many grocery stores and health food stores, if you don't have access to an Asian market. "Lite" coconut milk doesn't have the same health benefits as regular coconut milk, but it can be useful as a dairy substitute if you are sensitive to dairy and want to reduce the fat intake of your diet.

coconut oil:

Recent research has revealed that coconut oil has many healthful properties. It also only contains 6.8 calories per gram as opposed to other fat sources, which contain 9 calories per gram. I use the expeller-pressed coconut oil, but virgin coconut oil is an excellent product.

ground nuts:
Other than almonds, like hazelnuts, walnuts, pecans. They are all useful in baking as a flour alternative and are especially useful in quick breads and pie crusts.

guar gum:
see *xanthan gum*.

hot chili oil:
Hot chili oil is available at most grocery stores in the ethnic foods section. Please try to purchase hot sesame chili oil rather than hot chili oil made with other vegetable oils.

kefir:
Kefir is a wonderful fermented dairy product that has a host of healthful probiotics, not to mention the fact that it is delicious. Kefir is available at health food stores, but is best when "brewed" at home. Avoid the packets of starter culture, as they don't contain the entire complement of probiotics that are contained in kefir that has been brewed from "grains." Kefir grains are available from anyone who has them; they are generally free or are sold for the cost of postage. See Dom's Kefir In-Site in the Bibliography for more information.

lard:
I use lard because it is a natural, rather than man-made, fat source. I noticed immediate health benefits when I stopped using the typical liquid oils that are in most American homes. It is usually available in the meat aisle near the bacon or in the ethnic foods section with the Mexican food. Try to avoid hydrogenated lard, if at all possible.

lemon pepper:
Choose a variety that has no sugar or MSG. It is available in the seasonings section of grocery stores.

milk and egg protein powder:
A product found in the beverage aisle of many health food stores. The brand I use is labeled as Milk & Egg Protein Powder and contains calcium caseinate, milk protein isolate, whey protein isolate, DHA powder, egg white, soy lecithin, maltodextrin, natural flavor, bromelain, and papain. It has 1 gram of carbohydrates per ½ cup. It performs differently in baking than does soy protein isolate, which more closely resembles wheat flour in its behavior. Milk and egg protein is, however, more absorbent than soy protein isolate. Milk and egg protein doesn't convert 1:1 as soy protein isolate does for wheat flour in baking.

olive oil:
I generally use virgin olive oil, though in some recipes, you may wish to use "light" olive oil, which has a milder flavor than that of the virgin. I use olive oil in most applications where a liquid oil is called for. I don't prefer it for frying as it imparts a distinct flavor to foods, but some recipes do great with that flavor. This is just a personal preference.

other oils:
Walnut, peanut, and grape seed oils are very high in antioxidants and are good alternatives to the highly processed liquid oils like soybean and corn. Use them as your wallet dictates!

pork rinds, ground:

I purchase pork rinds in the Mexican foods section of my local grocery store. They also go by the name of *chicharrones,* and to put it very simply, are fried pork skin. They are a very high protein food, and are actually surprisingly low in both fat and sodium, considering that they are sold as a "chip." I grind my own to a fine powder using my food processor.

sea salt:

I use sea salt instead of regular table salt for its increased mineral content. It is available in most better stores. Beware of the brands that add sugar to their salt!

seasoning salt:

Choose a variety that has no sugar or MSG. It is available in the seasonings section of grocery stores.

sesame oil (roasted):

Sesame oil is available at most grocery stores in the ethnic foods section. It is less expensive and more choices are available at an Asian market.

SteviaPlus:

A blend of stevia (herb) and inulin fiber that is a great natural (not man-made) sweetener. It has no impact on blood sugar levels and can help promote a healthy digestive tract.

sucralose:

I use the brand Splenda No Calorie Sweetener in the packets. I don't use the granular form, in general, because it has a lot of filler, thus more empty carbs.

Sugar-free specialty syrups:

These are the type that are typically associated with flavored coffees. There are many brands on the market, just please do your best to avoid the ones made with aspartame, as that sweetener is not heat stable and is unsuitable for baking. The brands I use are Torani and DaVinci's. They are available at larger supermarkets and also through catalogs and Internet purchase.

Sweet & Slender:

A blend of fructose and luo han guo fruit extract. The fructose is the carrier for the intensely sweet luo han guo fruit. It isn't intensely sweet like sucralose or stevia, but has a comparatively mild sweet flavor. It is great in muffins, teas, and used as a flavor enhancer in recipes.

vital wheat gluten flour:

Vital wheat gluten is the protein portion of the wheat. This product is 75 percent protein. It contains 6 grams of carbohydrates per ¼ cup. It is excellent for baked goods because of its propensity for rising and producing an elastic dough. It is called vital wheat gluten or vital wheat gluten flour, and can be found in the baking aisle in most stores, usually on the top shelf with other specialty products.

xanthan gum:

Xanthan gum is a tiny microorganism that provides thickening and leavening qualities. It contains 8 grams of carbohydrates per tablespoon but is pure fiber so has no impact on blood glucose levels. I also use it as a binder in crusts that need extra support due to a very moist filling.

Substitutions for Ingredients Found in This Book

"But I can't find that ingredient!" Here's some help.

arrowroot powder:

You may substitute xanthan gum for arrowroot in sauces or gravies.

Bragg Liquid Aminos:

You may use soy sauce in place of Bragg Liquid Aminos. If you are allergic to soy, I've found a combination of lemon juice and seasoning salt will make an equitable substitution for soy sauce or Bragg Liquid Aminos.

coconut milk:

If you cannot locate coconut milk, you may substitute buttermilk or kefir in most recipes calling for coconut milk; however, the taste will be quite different.

coconut oil:

You may substitute olive oil or lard in most recipes calling for coconut oil.

kefir:

Buttermilk may be used for kefir in most recipes. In some recipes yogurt may be used equally for kefir.

lard:

Nothing fries food quite like lard does, but as a substitute you may use coconut oil or olive oil. Just be aware that the taste and finished product will be different when using these oils rather than lard.

lemon pepper:

If you can't find lemon pepper without sugar, you can use black pepper and a small amount of lemon zest.

milk and egg protein powder:

This one is harder to substitute, and will require experimentation in the specific recipe, but generally soy protein isolate or vital wheat gluten may be substituted for milk and egg protein.

olive oil:

Depending upon the recipe, melted butter can be substituted if it is being used in a baked good. If it is a fried food, you may use lard or coconut oil.

pork rinds, ground:

Again, changing this ingredient in a recipe will yield vastly different results than the original, but in most cases ground almonds or possibly soy protein isolate (depending upon the recipe) will work in place of ground pork rinds.

seasoning salt:

What if you can't find any seasoning salt without sugar or MSG? You can use garlic salt in its place with very little effect upon the recipe.

soy protein isolate:

You may use vital wheat gluten in place of soy protein isolate in baked goods. In protein shakes, you may use milk and egg protein powder instead of soy protein isolate.

soy sauce:

You may use Bragg Liquid Aminos in place of soy sauce. If you are allergic to soy, see Bragg Liquid Aminos.

SteviaPlus:

You may substitute other stevia products for SteviaPlus, but the results will vary from brand to brand. Refer to the chart provided for assistance in sweetness equivalencies (see page 251).

sucralose:

You may substitute SteviaPlus or Sweet & Slender for sucralose, or you may choose another favorite sweetener. Just beware of aspartame, as it isn't heat stable and is not suitable for cooking.

sugar-free specialty syrups:

You can substitute flavored extracts plus sweetener and some more liquid in recipes calling for these.

Sweet & Slender:

Since it isn't intensely sweet like sucralose or SteviaPlus, converting Sweet & Slender recipes will require a bit of finesse. There is a conversion chart provided in this book (see page 251).

vital wheat gluten flour

You may use soy protein isolate in place of vital wheat gluten.

xanthan gum:

Guar gum can be used or special blends of the gums can be purchased at specialty stores. In gravies and sauces, arrowroot powder may be used instead of xanthan gum. In baked goods, substitutions are more difficult. In many cases it may simply be omitted, but this will greatly affect the end product.

Bibliography

Dr. Atkins' New Diet Revolution
Go-Diet—The Goldberg-O'Mara Diet Plan. *http:// members.tripod.com/~himolocarb/*

Whole Soybeans. 8 October, 2003. Indiana Soybean Board. *www.soyfoods.com*

U.S. Soyfoods Directory. 4 December, 2003. Stevens & Associates, Inc. *www.soyfoods.com/soyfoodsdescriptions/ descriptions.html*

Wisdom Herbs: Products: Sweet Leaf. 4 December, 2003. Wisdom Natural Brands.
www.wisdomnaturalbrands.com

Bob's Red Mill—Whole Grain Foods for Every Meal of the Day. 4 December, 2003.
www.bobsredmill.com

Weight Loss. 4 December, 2003. Tropical Traditions.
www.tropicaltraditions.com

Dom's Kefir In-Site. 4 December, 2003. Dominic N. Anfiteatro.
http://users.chariot.net.au/~dna/kefirpage.html

Index